WINNING STRATEGIES FOR CAPITAL FORMATION

Secrets of Funding Start-Ups and Emerging Growth Firms without Losing Control of Your Idea, Project, or Company

LINDA CHANDLER

McGraw-Hill

New York San Francisco Washington, D.C. Auckland Bogotá
Caracas Lisbon London Madrid Mexico City Milan
Montreal New Delhi San Juan Singapore
Sydney Tokyo Toronto

McGraw-Hill

A Division of The McGraw·Hill Companies

This publication is designed to provide accurate and authoritative information in regard to the subject matter covered. It is sold with the understanding that neither the author or the publisher is engaged in rendering legal, accounting, or other professional service. If legal advice or other expert assistance is required,the services of a competent professional person should be sought.

From a Declaration of Principles jointly adopted by a Committee of the American Bar Association and a Committee of Publishers.

Library of Congress Cataloging-in-Publication Data

Chandler, Linda.
    Winning strategies for capital formation : secrets of funding
start-ups and emerging growth firms without losing control of your
idea, project, or company / Linda Chandler.
        p.   cm.
    Includes index.
    ISBN 0-7863-0892-3
    1. Venture capital.   I. Title.
HG4751.C436   1997
658.15'23—dc20   96–23790

Printed in the United States of America
    3 4 5 6 7 8 9 0 DO 3 2 1 0 9

Finding oneself short of the money to launch new ideas, ideas that burn brightly, that beg to be done, is a situation that reaches back as far as Christopher Columbus for Americans. When good ideas and their implementation are presented with passion, vision, clarity, and a reasonably likely plan to bring them about, the listener is convinced and the dollars to back the enterprise are forthcoming.

Outstanding entrepreneurs and their ideas are truly seductive to the capital markets. What makes for an outstanding entrepreneur? In this book I provide guidelines, not rules, that help you assess the answers to that question and help you achieve that status. Underlying it all, however, is a basic quality that defines those most likely to succeed, not merely in the financial sense but in the sense of personal and societal fulfillment.

Entrepreneurs most likely to find funding are those so driven by their belief and vision—in essence, their *passion*—that nothing and no one will stop them from tackling the challenge. Whether or not they will always be successful is not the issue. As they create or find ideas (opportunities) that they fall in love with and come to believe in absolutely, their passion and commitment to turn them into reality fills them with energy of virtually superhuman dimension.

The challenge of creating a real business out of an innovative idea moves them always forward. The operative words here—*always forward*—define the true entrepreneurial spirit. There is no such thing as failure. Setbacks certainly do occur. Mistakes, absolutely. Misdirection, underestimation, overzealousness—no doubt. But there is never permanent failure, only lessons to be learned, stored in the memory bank, and gleaned from in the next endeavor. This, after all, is a lifetime process.

In today's environment there are no rules—only guidelines—to creating success. In the global markets and world in which we now find ourselves, all business—from the smallest home-operated one to the largest conglomerate—must not only operate with innovation and creativity, but must also be lean and flexible, always with an eye to the future and implementation today that anticipates change.

No one is exempt from becoming an entrepreneur. In fact, there has never before been a time so ripe as this one. Today the doors are wide open to do what you absolutely love, find the backing to support your ideas (given they are, in fact, innovative, meet a serious and defined need for a significant audience, be it a niche or the mass), and create a life and a legacy of which to stand proud.

For some, the belief and passion in themselves is hidden deep, having been drummed out through an educational process. We have been taught to conform, to be more like a manager than a leader, to put others' ideas far ahead of our own. We have to shed that training.

Whether you are one of the bold, who exude self-confidence and bravado, or one of the timid, who are being forced from the nest of corporate parenting or who have reached the point of wanting to throw off the mantle of just doing something for a living to living to do something, it will take inordinate persistence and courage to begin and maintain your quest for entrepreneurial success. For many, it is learning to break the mold and believe enough in oneself to begin. Persistence and courage to forge ahead despite all obstacles are two of the most important qualities you will need and should continue to nourish.

The good news is that it is all doable. The core of the issue to become, be, and sustain your place as a successful entrepreneur is to get in touch with your dream and believe absolutely that it is within your power to turn that dream into reality. You can! The guidelines herein will assist you; they are techniques that work. It is up to you and you alone to live doing what you love and learn to keep doing it better and better along the way.

Best of luck! May my insights and coaching assist you in living your entrepreneurial dreams.

After you read this book, I would love to hear your comments and feedback. If this book helped you raise the capital, the resources and the partners you sought, please share your experience with me. That was the main purpose of writing this book.

You can write me, either c/o McGraw-Hill, Inc., or you can send your letters directly to the offices of Chandler Leadership & Development, Inc., P.O. Box 1360, Fernandina Beach, FL 32035-1360. E-mail: bizseminar@aol.com

I also welcome short stories and contributions describing your entrepreneurial journeys, challenges, breakthroughs, and triumphs. I am gathering background materials and stories for upcoming books focusing on examples of persistence, integrity, and guts.

Linda Chandler
Amelia Island, Florida

ACKNOWLEDGMENTS

No book is written entirely alone. The encouragement, advice, and input from mentors, business leaders, friends, colleagues, and associates from different walks of life have helped me create a book of which I am proud.

My sincere thanks to my mentors Dan Stephenson, Ken Green, Warren Berl, Glenn Jones, Steve Boyle, Denis Waitley, and Joe Foss.

Special appreciation to my New York literary agent, Nicholas Smith of Altair Literary Agency, and my outstanding team of editors at Irwin Professional, including Amy Ost, Patrick Muller, and Pamela Sourelis and Jim Labeots.

For their enthusiastic encouragement, input, time, and wisdom, I also sincerely thank Ko Hayashi, Bobbie Dhaemers, Al Cummings, Terry Chandler, Venu and Linda GoPaul, Edwin and Fely Smith, Ann and Chuck Hurley, Patti and Ray Hallstein, David Neenan, Peter Morris, Scott DeGarmo, David T. Allen, Roger McManus, David and Carol Andrews, Suzanne and Bill Edmark, Maria Duncan, Jerry Chang, Henry Chen, Gail Larsen, Jerry Perniece, Dona Lock, Gaile Sickel, Kay Snow-Davis, Elorian Landers, M. J. Maday, David Jokinen, Dub McNamara, Carolyn Lundy, Richard Collins, Mark Collins, Thomas Wright, Gary and Yvonne Daniels, Pualani Chandler and family, Pam Black, Jade Smith, Audrey Fu, Diedre Jersey, Cam Cooper, Candy Alexander, Elaine Willis, Peg Jordan, Sharan Ro, Moto Eguchi, Bob Mills, Paul Gilman, Wally Minto, Barbara Altemus, Elsha Bohnert, Joe and Pat Wyman, Martha Bates, Betty and Warren Hard, Bob Goodale, Grant Holcomb, Brian Petula, Yolanda Batts, Bill Williams, James Nolen, Cynthia Dinkins, Sanchiro Uchida, Joyce Shepherd, Sigrid Laing, Paul Hayashi, Pat and Ursula Medlen, Irene Peterson, Robert Donnan, Lynda Fogle, Betsy Wallace, B. K. Nelson, Sonia Reedy, Mark Duncan, Ed Sweeney, Star Mathias, Cal Yonamine, Lorna Henry, Carolyn and Andy Svorinic, Alexandra and Gene Abrams, John and Sheri Hieber, Diane and Donald Lee, Shaun McCoy, Ken Kirby, Michael Webb, Virginia Weber, Vicki and Okky Oei, Terek and Adam Diasti, Gerald Thomason, Paul Barton, Paula Petrovic, Terry Allen, Eden Kim, Kim Christianson, Ken Eller, Laura Weiss, Helmut Gieben, and M. J. and Michael Clarke.

And to my family—my Mother, my Father, my Brother Mark, my Aunts, Winifred and Lucy, and Uncles Neal and Bob, Cheryl, April, Tim, and Paul—thank you for your abiding love and belief.

ALSO BY LINDA CHANDLER

It's Just a K.I.S.S. Away: A Woman's Guide to Winning the Money Game
ISBN 0-9639400-0-7   Learning 2000 Press (Softcover Book)

Secrets of Raising Serious Money for Your Business—Part 1 (Audio Album)
ISBN 0-9639400-1-5   Learning 2000 Audio (Entrepreneurship Series)

Secrets of Raising Serious Money for Your Business—Part 2 (Audio Album)
ISBN 0-9639400-3-1   Learning 2000 Audio (Entrepreneurship Series)

Compelling Selling: Pathways to Sales Mastery (Audio Album)
ISBN 0-9639400-5-1   Learning 2000 Audio (Sales Mastery Series)

Sales Magic: The Seven Principles of Sales Mastery (Audio Album)
ISBN 0-9639400-4-x   Learning 2000 Audio (Sales Mastery Series)

STOP! If you're hunting for valuable information on entrepreneurship, if you want to experience its highs and avoid its perils and pitfalls, do yourself a favor and make a firm commitment to read *Winning Strategies for Capital Formation.*

Why do I feel so strongly about this? Let me tell you about the turmoil my friend Mike has been through in his entrepreneurial career. If only he'd been able to read this excellent book years ago.

Mike created his first successful company when he was barely 20 years old. In that venture, he was a true pioneer. Unfortunately, he tried to model his subsequent companies after that early success. Had he read this book, he would have understood why being a pioneer is often not the great advantage one perceives it to be. He drove his next big venture up to nearly $50 million in sales before it became plagued with problems. Before its crash, the enterprise was written up in the press as being hot, and coverage about Mike in the national, local, and trade media hailed him as an innovator and visionary.

No one could deny Mike had his share of brilliance, intuition, and entrepreneurial insight. But on repeated occasions his life became a tangle of lawsuits, indebtedness, and roller-coaster swings in personal wealth that took him to the brink of impoverishment. At one point I spoke with him in the basement of one of his relative's houses, where he holed up while fending off a deluge of angry creditors and legal assaults.

Having the opportunity to read this book makes you much luckier than Mike. And I urge you to read it from beginning to end, a request I don't make lightly; I know that entrepreneurial types excel at scouring, and scanning, and zeroing in on the information that they need *now*—but that's exactly my point. The sooner you assimilate the overview presented in these pages, the better. I make that point because of Mike. His maneuvers were often wonders to behold. But all too often they were desperate tactics aimed at just staying alive. The perception and farsightedness that enabled him to think of exciting products and marketing schemes gave him little in the way of understanding the entrepreneurial process. He had no map, no larger frame of reference. He viewed all events through the fog of battle, seeing just a step or two ahead.

If you are just starting on your journey, or wondering if you have enough entrepreneurial blood in your veins to take the first step, this book will provide you with the panorama that Mike never had. It will also help you assess your fitness for the adventure. (Mike was full of blind spots about his own strengths and weaknesses. He thought he was a great manager; in fact, his skills in that area were suitable only for the early stages of a venture.) If you are already a seasoned traveler, your appreciation should be all the keener, for you'll recognize in Linda Chandler an astute guide who knows the entire territory, from the major trails to the obscure crossings and passages.

The theme that permeates the book bears restating: To be a successful entrepreneur invariably means learning a lot about raising capital.

I recall Mike's frustration when it came to getting reliable advice about capital formation. Hours of technical input from lawyers, accountants, and other specialists often left him more baffled than when he began. Often he was tripped up because many of those from whom he sought counsel had their own agendas and their own limitations, as Chandler makes clear.

Once, while waiting for Mike, I spent a few hours looking at the stack of books on entrepreneurship in his office. When Mike finally showed up, I told him the books made me think of the Hippocratic oath doctors are required to take: First, do no harm. The truth is that much writing on entrepreneurship is so laden with incomplete or misleading information that, at the very least, it is a waste of time—and time is a resource that Mike and all entrepreneurs always find to be in short supply. As Mike sprawled on his couch, recovering from a brutal day of rejection, I passed the time by holding up each of the books I'd been examining and offering a brief assessment. Some were egregiously self-serving; these were typically composed of supposedly colorful war stories and favorite anecdotes that had been pushed into procrustean beds and tortured for lessons that turned out to be elusive at best. Going through the other books sent us careening from the superficial, to the academic, and into the arms of the irrelevant. The reader, like Mike, thirsting for insight and information, would eventually find himself asking, "But where are the principles, concepts, techniques, and insights that apply to *me*."

If I seem to flail away at such books a bit too fervently, I do so simply because reading *Winning Strategies for Capital Formation* reminds me of how much value a good book *can* deliver. The lessons in this book do indeed apply to you, if you're now an entrepreneur or intend to become one. If this had been one of the books in Mike's office, I sincerely believe many events could have gone differently for him.

Mike's struggles with business plans are a case in point. Helping entrepreneurs write business plans has become an industry of its own, with products ranging from dazzling interactive offerings to spiral-bound notebooks in which you fill in the blanks. Chandler provides more insight in several of her paragraphs on business plan writing than I have seen revealed in entire books on the subject (not to mention software programs and CD-ROMs). At last, one starts to understand the essence of the matter—there are *many* uses for business plans, and the entrepreneur needs to master all of them. As to the issue of when a business plan is finished, the answer is simple: Never.

I also wish Mike could have learned about investors from Chandler. The hit-or-miss manner in which he acquired his knowledge often proved disastrous. In this book, you will meet the different types of investors—a veritable taxonomy of investors, from the good species you will want on your team to the ones you should avoid like poisonous mushrooms (see Chapter 6). In your entrepreneurial career you may encounter them all. Chandler describes each and helps you tell them apart. You will learn how to locate them (Chapter 7) and how to make presentations suitable for each species. Without ever prescribing a rigid formula (rigidity is not what you need in this game), Chandler breaks down the type of presentation required into minutes and *seconds*. She tells you how to be alert to the questions that are going through investors' minds when you are speaking to them, and just what questions *you* should be asking *them*. She also tells you what to do *after* the presentation.

I am sure Mike still smarts when he recalls one April day in New York. His team had prepared assiduously and then performed with great credibility during the presentation—only to watch their own progress disintegrate for lack of understanding of how to follow up. They had gone out of their way to learn about what went into a good presentation, but from an expert in presentations—not capital formation. In this book you get both brands of expertise (Chapter 8).

In short, Chandler has been through it all enough times to be able to tell you what lies around the bend. She tells you how to keep the next step in mind while succeeding in the present. (Come to think of it, isn't that the indelible mark of a winner?) She has the gift of being able to remember the simple stumbling blocks that trip up the novice, while holding in mind the high-level intricacies that await you further down the path. She also manages to combine all the various perspectives—legal, financial, managerial—into a unified whole.

The book is also a pleasure to read. When an author is as immersed in her fields as Chandler is, the result can be a natural eloquence that stems not from any conscious effort at wordsmithery, but from having mastered the subject matter in all its complexity and being able to speak confidently without squeamish qualifications. The pages are studded with aphoristic turns of phrase that provide insight and discernment: "Prior experience is one thing," Chandler reminds us. "Successful entrepreneurial accomplishment is quite another."

Mike's love of pithy statements and quotations would have made this book's lessons hit home with him. He would have noted the forceful recommendation that the entrepreneur keep focused "on the ultimate goal—that of selling early stage equity for a substantial profit in some fashion at some point in the foreseeable future." In fact, when it came to exit strategies, Mike never gave them much thought; certainly he did not realize the importance of thinking about them early in the life of each new venture, which is one of the "secrets" Chandler reveals. As she sums up, "the nearer you get to the time of exit, the less flexibility in the options available to you."

Of course, this book wasn't written when Mike was starting his ventures—an obvious point I make to emphasize the timeliness of its information, which includes illuminating insights into the most recent and celebrated IPOs. Chandler draws her knowledge from an immensely rich background. Her anecdotes are expertly chosen, with an eye to enlightening the reader, not telling war stories or crowing about her connections and experience in venture capital (though she has a great deal to crow about, having been present at the creation of some of the country's most noted entrepreneurial enterprises). Because of her multifaceted understanding, Chandler is able to map the ups and downs of raising capital in a way that spreads the entire landscape before you, offering both macro and micro perspectives. At any step along the way, you'll see the choices you have to make and the various paths open to you. She combines a grand overview of the capital raising process with astute observations about the people and situations you'll encounter.

A few final words about Mike. In the popular press he went from being lauded as an exciting leader to being plastered with such labels as obsessively controlling. His failures often got attributed to personality flaws or some psychological deficiency. I don't quite believe that. Certainly, in the midst of some of the worst crises he got pretty rattled, but then he was facing losses in the tens of millions of dollars. Who wouldn't get upset? I think, though, what did him in was lack of sophistication about the entrepreneurial process. He relied on his technical savvy, creativity, and energy, but those weren't enough to get him very far, especially in a field of increasingly savvy players.

The good news for Mike is that the time is ripe for him to make a rebound. He's got a new idea he's working on, and it sounds like it could be a hot one. You can bet I am going to make sure he reads this book before he gets too far.

The good news for you is that *Winning Strategies for Capital Formation* is written with energy, passion, intelligence, and respect for the reader. It is exciting and enormously inspiring without ever raising false expectations. It gives a clear sense of what can and must be done and is thus the highest form of motivation. I suggest you think of it in terms of return on investment: The few hours you spend reading these pages will yield rewards far into the future.

Scott DeGarmo
Editor-In-Chief
Success Magazine

BRIEF CONTENTS

CONTENTS

Chapter 3

Building Credibility by Building a Business Plan That Clearly Represents Your Business   45

Chapter 4

Financials That Actually Mean Something   67

CHAPTER 1

Preparing Yourself for the Money Hunt

When you go out to raise money for your project, you need to be really focused and determined to succeed. As a developer of real estate projects, I needed to accurately target and pinpoint the movement and cycles of the real estate market along with interest rate and money market patterns. When asked what is the key to my success, I answer that it is a total belief that I can accomplish whatever I set out to do. I learned that from my father. He inspired me to believe that I had the right stuff to do extraordinary things.

Jeanne A. Anderson
Real Estate Developer (Hawaii)

Whether you are truly an entrepreneur ready to launch or grow your business or a small business owner contemplating using outside capital to help you, entering into the "money hunt" is an interesting challenge. For most, it is entering into a world of possibilities that may be foreign to anything experienced.

The process of getting OPM (Other People's Money) into backing you and your endeavor is one that intimidates many, be they existing business magnates or wet-behind-the-ears newbies. For most, it is looked upon as a necessary evil and something to get through as quickly as   possible.

Nonetheless, unless your family can and will back your ideas as far as you (and they) can take them, or you have ties to the Rockefeller or Mellon families, the search for outside funds becomes an important part of growing your business. There often comes a point at which you have exhausted all your personal and family resources and you must begin to look further. This is when you begin a money hunt in earnest.

The other option you always have is to continue to capitalize from within. This alternative is usually the slower, more paced approach to growing the business. Unfortunately in the business environment of today, taking such time may not be a luxury you can afford if your business is rapidly changing or facing fierce competition. Nevertheless, you may still conclude at the end of this treatise that the time, the energy, and the cost of searching for outside funds is simply not worth it . . . at least to you!

Seeking capital to launch or fuel ideas is not a new idea. Understanding, *truly understanding,* the ways and means to go about it that make the most sense for your particular enterprise and the people who comprise it *is* (a somewhat revolutionary idea, that is). The more you come to understand about this process, the better that knowledge can serve you and everyone involved with your endeavor!

The most important first step to beginning the hunt is to determine for yourself whether you are an entrepreneur or a small business person. The reason this is important to understand is that entrepreneurs are a different breed from small business owners. Neither is better than the other; they are merely different. Because these personality types as well as ultimate objectives *are* different, the how, when, who, and what of putting together a workable approach to getting that OPM are all affected.

The objective of doing business is normally defined quite differently, depending on who is doing the defining, whether it be an entrepreneur or a self-employed business person. Their views on many important business matters are often worlds apart, including how they look at money, its cost, use, and value. Those people who see themselves as business owners, as apart from entrepreneurs, normally have no intention of leaving their business. Entrepreneurs, on the other hand, more often than not like to get their idea into creation, get it up and running, and then personally move on to other things, start something new, something fresh.

Entrepreneurs might best be defined as visionaries. Small business owners as managers/operators. Both have elements of one another's strengths as well as weaknesses but have a basic overriding difference in style and goals. So, which definition fits you best?

The primary reasons for the confusion about the use of the term "entrepreneur" are twofold. One is that the term today is one of the buzzwords of the times, carrying with it an implication of unbridled genius and/or potential for wealth. In other words, everyone wants to be one.

The other reason for some confusion is that the term is tossed around with unstated or understated implications by the users, depending on their own interpretations or experience. Thus, you may consider yourself to be one and others do not, or the other way around.

The definition of an entrepreneur as provided by Webster is:

> One who organizes, manages, and assumes the risks of a business or enterprise.

This is not a bad definition to use as our baseline. All three elements—taking the risk, organizing it, and then managing it—are fundamental to creating and operating a successful enterprise.

ENTREPRENEURS CREATE RATHER THAN REACT

Entrepreneurs are those individuals who seek truly innovative solutions rather than mere alterations. Entrepreneurs create rather than merely react to the outside stimuli affecting their endeavors. Entrepreneurs seek to achieve; they accomplish task after task and build on each accomplishment, always leading to new and challenging opportunities. Entrepreneurs set goals for themselves and their organization, raising the standards of performance and excellence.

Entrepreneurs manage existing resources effectively while seeking new knowledge and solutions that may not even exist in the present.

Whatever their innate intelligence and/or training, they constantly seek to upgrade their knowledge. They surround themselves with people who raise, rather than lower, the standards they set for themselves and their organization.

In this world where the very nature of change alters midcourse, to say nothing of the rate at which it comes at us, each of us is forced to acknowledge our need to go beyond coping to leadership. Because of the integral relationship between leadership and learning, the true leaders among us are constantly in a state of learning. Entrepreneurs personify this leadership.

ENTREPRENEURS ARE MODERATE RISK TAKERS

They are not afraid to take risks. They realize that to grow, one must take risks. Because there is no such thing as status quo, especially in the world of change in which we find ourselves today, the only risk is in not taking any. Thus, entrepreneurs demonstrate their courage in the face of fear by taking educated action.

They rarely act in a vacuum, though. Entrepreneurs learn the art of communication and apply it well. They communicate with others to achieve alignment and commitment from all parties to the particular challenge. Then, when they do proceed, they accept the responsibility for their actions, no matter the outcome.

Entrepreneurs grasp the concept that what they are actively doing today is playing out their part, a very important piece of a very large puzzle. They have the ability to see beyond the day-to-day activity to conceptualize the global picture, knowing all the while the importance of each step, each player. For those individuals and companies seeking more than mere survival, learning and applying strategies that are in alignment with the underlying philosophy and purpose of the founders is the best guarantee for lasting success.

Entrepreneurs have the confidence to find the resources they need, be they people, knowledge, or capital. This intrinsic quality sets entrepreneurs apart and defines their capabilities.

In just this last decade the definition and perception of who is and who is not an entrepreneur has changed drastically. Well into the 1980s entrepreneurs were nearly always described in the following terms:

Young (25 to 35 years old).

Male (well, an occasional exception).

Majority Caucasian and heterosexual.

Inherited the belief that "he or she with the most toys wins!"

Lifestyle unpretentious (lack of emphasis on style, more on substance in residence, dress, appearance, relationships).

Does things fast (eat, sleep, drive, think).

Spends *every waking moment* devoted to the DREAM.

More often than not divorced (see above description for cause and effect).

Lives in urban, high-growth area.

Liberal political leanings (although not much direct involvement).

Dreads possibility of having to actually *manage* long-term anything
(including growth of the corporation).

My! How times they are a-changing! Whether through necessity in these final years of the 20th century or just a total awakening, entrepreneurs today are people in all walks of life, of both genders, virtually *all* ages, races, geographic locations, and lifestyles. Perhaps the greatest secret of all, shared only with our fellow entrepreneurs is this:

> *The rate of change in the world today and in all of our tomorrows demands of us the development and practice of entrepreneurial skills, no matter our role at home or in the office, no matter our gender, race, spiritual beliefs, or station in life. This is the dawning of a new age. We are all budding and blooming with new ideas, new solutions, and moving into new dimensions.*

The following characteristics are the ones I feel best define those business people who are successful, be they typically defined as entrepreneurs or not. Most individuals described by these characteristics do see themselves as entrepreneurs or as leaders of the business revolution at hand.

Successful entrepreneurs:

- Are creative and innovative in their problem solving.

- Get things done and build upon their achievements.

- Set goals for performance.

- Maximize resources in all ways.
- Seek understanding and greater, deeper knowledge (wisdom).
- Demonstrate leadership through the learning process.
- Exhibit courage by taking "educated" risks.
- Accept responsibility for their actions.
- Communicate well.
- Are team players who work in cooperation with others.
- Have vision beyond the scope of today.
- Are happy being just exactly who they are.
- Have confidence in their abilities, themselves, and their purpose.

Businesses, large and small, are founded and, at least initially, led by one or more entrepreneurs whose philosophies and purpose permeate the very fabric of the organization. The more people within any organization who share the purpose and philosophy and incorporate the qualities of entrepreneurship, the greater the likelihood for lasting success.

ASKING THE TOUGH QUESTIONS

Tough Question One: Control

Once you have determined whether you are an entrepreneur or a self-employed business person you are ready to begin on your journey to bag the money. This is the time to address some of the tough questions that will come up during the "capital hunt." The first among them is where you stand on the issue of control of your organization, its ideas and people.

All would-be capital hunters should understand that the earlier in the game they go in pursuit of outside funds, the more likely they are to end up *being controlled* rather than *controlling* the destiny of the project, enterprise, or company. If you are the lead entrepreneur, you are probably the one who, at least for a time, will be in charge of day-to-day decisions. That is certainly one important measure of control.

Determining the destiny of the organization is quite different, however. The one who sets the course for the ship may or may not be the one steering the ship on a daily basis. This destiny will increasingly be determined by those who hold the critical purse strings or, at a minimum, access to them.

It is wise to remember that the earlier you bring in equity partners, the more equity you, as founder(s), give up. The result of giving up equity early is that you are highly likely to retain only a tiny percentage of the company when what you consider to be the ultimate reward (going public through an initial public offering comes about).

Because the average number of rounds of financing for most successful companies before the initial public offering (IPO) is between three and six, each time the pie gets cut, it will be your share that gets reduced. Now, that may be good news or not. It's the equivalent of being a small frog in a very large pond or a large frog in a very small one. It is the value of the pond that determines the financial reward.

Understanding this, the determination of seeking and accepting outside funding takes on a new dimension. You, as the lead entrepreneur, project leader, or founder of the company, have the task of evaluating whether the outside funding can create a more valuable company in a shorter time period. That is the crux of the decision relative to "giving up" control of the organization. For many, many entrepreneurs that control issue is the *big* stumbling block.

Wrestling with this issue of control is perhaps the most difficult issue you and your co-founders and early managers not only will begin with but also will come back to time and time again throughout your expansion. You may consider yourself to be in charge so long as you or someone you direct is CEO of the corporation. This is not necessarily true.

You may consider yourself or yourself along with your co-founders to be in control so long as you are the majority stockholders of the company. Again, not necessarily. You may think control is in your hands because you "control" the board of directors. Once again, many a company's founder has found a nasty surprise by making this assumption.

A case in point is the following story related to me by Wilson Harrell, founder of *Inc.* magazine and numerous entrepreneurial companies:

How A CEO Found Himself Voted Out

The CEO of a publicly traded company on the NASDAQ (National Association of Securities Dealers over-the-counter market) found himself in the position of heading a company with sales in the $140 million range, showing continued stability and reasonable growth but with somewhat lackluster performance in the financial marketplace. The stock was trading at $13 per share, at a ho-hum price/earnings (P/E) ratio of 10.

His objective was to reconstitute the board, mount a campaign to promote the company to existing stockholders, and bring on board an impressive investment banking house. In short, his intention was to improve the value of the company for all.

At the board meeting, things did not go *exactly* the way he had planned. Because he did not have any long-term contract with the company either as CEO or as board member, the board voted to remove him and other members of his family. This was accomplished despite their majority stockholder position and family history of founding and heading the company since inception.

Alas! Control is in the hands of the party or parties who are directing the business to the destiny they have determined most viable and feasible. Normally, this is somewhat related to the highest financial reward they believe can be achieved and the time frame in which they ideally desire it to occur.

If the objectives of the directing parties are different from your own, the time to best determine that is at the beginning of your relationship with them. Those objectives need to reviewed, too, at every important stage in the growth and additional financing of your company. This can be accomplished only by keeping the lines of communication open and clear. A gentle reminder is this:

> The first time you bring in so much as one dollar from an outside party, you no longer are in sole "control" of the destiny of the enterprise.

Tough Question Two: Who Do You Want to Marry?

One important part of preparing for the capital hunt is learning this fundamental fact of life: *Not all money is the same.* If you have circled the wagons and feel the siege is under way, you are probably much less picky about the source of the funding or the terms that will come with it. Such desperation will cost you more sometimes than you understand at the time.

Thus, the key is to determine with forethought, well in advance of any real need, whether this OPM is the best choice for you. Giving yourself and your co-founders or initial managers space and time to think through the pros and cons of your alternatives will allow you to make a better choice of marital partners.

Yes. I did say marital partners. That is the best description I have found to date to describe the relationship into which you will enter with a funding source.

Now is the time to determine not only how much you want from them but who your sought-after candidates for funding might be. Realizing this is only the first round of capital (well, let's hope so, because if not, it means you are already in trouble!), you become aware that you will be back to the well a number of times before reaching the financial nirvana of going public.

Thinking the whole process through now puts you in the driver's seat to look around for candidates you want to be with you at every turn and who have the capability to do so. The alternative is multiple and changing partners at each level. This fact of life for many companies can become a nightmare.

Tough Question Three: How Are You Going to Spend the Money?

In these quiet moments before the chaos of building the project or company gets totally out of control, you and your management team can assess the best application of funds you seek. After all, you want to apply them in a fashion that will create the greatest and/or quickest boost to the over-all plan of the operation and ultimately create the greatest good for the greatest number of critical players.

Knowing all that, now you can concentrate on the plan to find the funding sources that match *your* wish list. You do have one, don't you? You know . . . the one that has all of the characteristics you most desire in a good partner and mate. The one that more or less follows a plan the way you see it unfolding. If not, there is no time like the present to create it.

Begin by listing what it is you want, in terms of "now" money, "future" money, and why. Then, list the qualities you seek in the people attached to that capital, both personal characteristics and professional help or guidance.

Then, finally, superimpose this "financial plan" on top of the one you have prepared to make the business work (the business plan). The how, when, where, and why of funds needed to get to each plateau as you progress will clarify for you and for the funding sources what you are likely to need and how you intend to apply it.

Once you complete this wish list in the form of a financial plan for the business you are better prepared to go about convincing the "right" sources that it is a mutually beneficial opportunity you are presenting.

This is your best chance as well as the best time to bring in the funds and the entity or entities to which those funds are attached under terms you both can conclude are optimum.

INTERPORE INTERNATIONAL

I believe this story of a California company is one of the best for all entrepreneurs, whether on their first or their hundredth "hunt," to take to heart. I include it here to prepare you for the hunt. Learning these lessons will allow you to achieve more consistent success in all you undertake. Preparing yourself this way is precisely what will allow you to "win the game" once *you* are in the arena.

Interpore International began in 1977 with leading-edge technology providing synthetic bone materials with application in the dental and medical fields, a crack management team, very good and virtually unbreakable patents, and a five-year history of successful beta site testing. On top of all this, the company was the sole source of the product developed.

In 1977 the company sublicensed the technology to Johnson & Johnson for $150,000 a year with a four-year contract. This sublicense provided much-needed cash flow to the company and set the stage for what the founders believed would become a working relationship to enhance and grow the market for their products. By 1981, the last year of the sublicense agreement, the company had only $100,000 left and decided to try to go public. The attempt failed and left the company $20,000 poorer for the effort.

In 1982 the founders decided to offer a limited partnership investment opportunity to health care professionals (those who would most easily understand the breakthrough solution provided by their company and the investment opportunity inherent therein). Again, the offering was not completed. It cost them an additional $30,000 for the attempt.

Later that same year the first serious venture capital group stepped forward and offered $1.2 million for 55 percent of the company. The anticipation was that the company would be brought to the public markets through an IPO within five years. By 1984 an additional $7.6 million was needed to continue the growth of the company. The same venture group came forth, again, expecting no more than a three- to five-year time frame for the public offering.

To secure this much-needed capital, the founders gave up an additional 29 percent of the company.

In 1987 the firm reached an agreement with a Japanese firm for cross-licensing and brought in an additional $2 million in exchange for the agreement and 1 percent of the company. (They were to learn in subsequent years that little was done to further corporate growth in the Japanese market. Eight years were to pass with virtually no significant results.)

Also in the late 1980s the firm acquired an orthopedic company. The strategy was to expand the product line and strengthen the positioning for ultimate value of the company.

By 1990 the firm required additional capital but was not yet considered ready through either positioning, visibility, or liquidity to go public. Once again the venture group stepped up to the table with an additional $5 million. In exchange, the group received another 5 percent of the corporate equity. A year later another $3.6 million was required, and the venture group ponied up for the last time in exchange for another 2 percent of the company.

Finally, in 1993 the company successfully launched its public offering for $13 million, absorbing yet another 3 percent of the remaining equity in the corporation. Founders and key principals were left with only 5 percent equity in the enterprise.

At this point the venture group had invested nearly $17.4 million. The "value" of the company at this juncture was approximately $33 million. This is *not* what venture groups consider to be a "home run"!

Dr. Edwin Shors, who served Interpore as executive vice president in the formative years, becoming head of research and development in 1983, remained the critical player throughout the process. When Dr. Shors left as the director of the Harbor/UCLA Medical Center thoracic and cardiovascular laboratory to join this leading-edge medical products company, little did he know it would be a nearly 17-year odyssey to take the company to the public market.

Questions these founders answered that are "standard, traditional" benchmarks for success were not enough. Yes, they passed muster by satisfying the traditional requirements. But they learned there were other questions they should have asked but did not. Here are some they asked after the fact that can help you now:

Yes, their product was unique.
   The questions they should have asked were:
   "How important was that to the world, the existing world of customers and the new world of developing customers?
   What would it take to get the customers to seek a newer, improved procedure?"

Yes, the size of the marketplace was enormous.
   The questions they should have asked were:
   "What was a reasonable time frame in which to capture it?
   Were their expectations realistic in scope and time?"

Yes, broadening the product base was a good idea.
   The questions they should have asked were:
   "Did the acquisition fit—geographically, personality, philosophically, and product compatability-wise? Did the use of resources emphasize the strengths of both or create a diversion? Were the decisions done for business reasons or for value reasons?"

Yes, one venture partner remained part of the "group" throughout the more than 10-year process.

The questions they should have asked were:

"From the very beginning (round 1), would the lead investor group remain in that position? What other venture groups did they have relationships with and would they pursue in future rounds of financing? What were the objectives of the different groups? Were their objectives compatible with the founders and with one another?"

Yes, the decisions were, by and large, sound.

The questions they should have asked were:

"Were circumstances beyond their control critical to the timing and success of the corporate growth? Just how much of their expectations hinged on such outside influences (i.e., FDA approvals)? Did creating two hurdles (two products, two companies) in place of one hamper product introduction and sales?"

Yes, the decision to take the company public was sound.

The question they should have asked was:

"Did the corporate insiders understand what would be required to achieve successful funding and support in the process?"

As stated earlier, desperate need for funds drives companies and their leaders to desperate measures. The only way I know of to avoid at least some of those desperate moments is by planning well in advance, understanding when and where the setbacks and hurdles are likely to come, and having a game plan to deal with them.

Desperation is nothing more or less than perception. Desperation is a reaction to feeling backed into a corner, with few places to turn.

When the "capital hunter" feels desperation for funding, it is usually out of fear. This fear is caused by either what may appear to be total exhaustion of resources at hand to the entrepreneur and his or her team, undercapitalization at critical junctures in the product's or company's evolvement, or a situation created unexpectedly through untimely surprises.

Tough Question Four: How Will We Maximize the Capital?

Because business expansion is thwarted more often by lack of funds than for any other reason, learning to do a capital hunt well is a talent worth cultivating. To do it well, the successful business owner or entrepreneur must learn how to maximize every dollar.

The timing, cost, and application of those dollars cannot be considered casually. Selecting the most appropriate structure and style of capital infusion is an additional consideration critical to the long-term plan for the organization. These detailed elements to the capital you seek *and will ultimately accept* are important.

Understanding their application to your particular endeavor will make an enormous difference in both the financial and emotional outcomes to you, as founders and management team, as well as to your investing partners. While we will investigate structure in a later chapter, suffice it to say here that structure can and does have a significant impact on how the capital can best be maximized for growth.

Maximizing every dollar and every resource is a strategy applied with keen ability by many of today's business leaders, small or large. Stretching dollars that don't even appear to exist is the domain of the "bootstrapper." *Bootstrapping* is a way of life for many, a useful operating tool at times for virtually all business owners.

Tough Question Five: Better to Bootstrap or use OPM?

Bootstrappers are those business owners or managers who reach down into their boots, find little but scraps of leather, yet strap those tattered and worn sections together to create a passable and workable "shoe" to get them on the road. Making up a large and growing segment of the entrepreneurial population, they and their methods are the stuff of which legends are made.

This name badge implies a certain frugality and creativity. Rightly so. *Bootstrappers* maximize opportunities for their business growth through all means at hand that allow them to stretch the resources within their grasp to maximum benefit.

Bootstrappers are adept at trading services, leveraging internal and external resources, and creating alliances whenever possible to form enterprises larger than their own resources would otherwise allow. They seize upon opportunities others often see only as problems or failures. They put the emphasis in their organizations on expenditures that create the greatest good for the least amount of effort or capital resources.

THE GLENN JONES STORY

My friend Glenn Jones, for whom I raised significant sums of investor funds for more than 10 years, is a prime example of bootstrapping beginnings leading to successful, enormous accomplishment. As a young attorney seeking his entrée into the business world, Glenn had as assets his degree, a used Volkswagen, and his entrepreneurial skills.

Glenn's dream was to create a network of cable television operating systems, develop technology for delivery and programming that would allow worldwide, real-time information transfer, interactive information exchange, and capabilities for data usage that would change the way people lived their day-to-day lives.

His dream was clearly bigger than his budget! But, as the visionary that he was and is to this day, Glenn realized he would not accomplish the goal overnight, easily, or without risk. He took on this elephant (his dream) with a knife and fork, by taking one bite at a time. His first bite was to get started with his first operating system.

Thus, Glenn purchased his first system in Georgetown, Colorado, for $12,000. He did not have $12,000. What he did have was his creative genius, courage, and determination. He persuaded the sellers to take $1,000 down and carry the $11,000 on a note. To get the $1,000, he borrowed $400 against his Volkswagen. The balance he collected from accounts receivable due from system subscribers.

A month later he purchased his second system in Idaho Springs, Colorado. Here he needed a technician. Who better than the prior owner? He convinced him to stay on in this capacity and together they strung cable from telephone poles. From these humble beginnings, Glenn built a company that today is one of the largest cable television operators in the United States. He serves as chairman of the board for the company he founded. Jones Intercable, Inc., ultimately raised more than $2.5 billion to fuel its growth and today owns 44 cable systems, operating in 20 states.

If you have the mind-set of a *bootstrapper,* you will utilize every means at your disposal before you will even consider bringing in outside capital to share in the wealth. In fact, many successful *bootstrappers* never do. Whether or not that becomes a limiting factor to growth depends on (1) the resources uncovered and (2) the ability to get the company to significant cash flow early, maintain that positive cash flow, and leverage off of it.

Most *bootstrappers* who grow their businesses on their own, without outside funding, do so because they have available to them enough capital and other key resources, including people, to sustain the operation to the point of achieving healthy, consistent cash flow. Achieving this level of internal cash generation is often called a "cash cow."

For most new businesses, divisions, and projects, reaching this point does not come easily or early. Generally, cash cows are projects or companies at a mature level with a developed customer base and a built-in barrier to entry to competition. Thus, for most young businesses, such internal capitalization is unlikely to be sustained.

In the Other Corner, Entrepreneurs Who Utilize OPM

Bootstrappers are only one breed of successful entrepreneurs. Another is the entrepreneur who effectively utilizes OPM. The primary difference here is that outside capital substitutes for leveraged or cleverly negotiated resources. Often the same resources are sought, or at least the same *type* of resources. It is the path to getting them that differs.

The energy and time of the business owners who go in search of OPM are put into the hunt for capital resources rather than negotiating a variety of what may be complex or tangled contracts and alliances. This is the route they have selected to solve the challenges facing their particular corporate survival and expansion. The skills of the founders, including resources at their command, play an important part in this decision.

Timing, too, is often an issue. How they see the application of their own time and energy, as well as that of their key managers and supporters, leads business expansionists to determine whether they will choose one route over another or will work to develop both forms simultaneously.

All business owners, leaders, and managers are faced with the dilemma of having only one even playing ground on which they compete (time available in any given day). The utilization of that time to capture any and all necessary resources required to enhance the timetable and expansion capability of the business is a core decision every participant must make.

The choice of *bootstrapping,* whether for a short period or for as long as possible, versus bringing in outside money and the parties to which it is attached is a constant dilemma facing virtually all businesses. This ongoing struggle for resources most useful to the company (time and money and how best to get it) does not go away once a company has passed the initial entrepreneurial stage of capital infusion. Decisions must be made time and time again on when, how much, and who are candidates to bring into the business in the form of capital contribution and participation.

Resources currently available, as well as those that can be acquired, can and will expand to fit the needs of the business. Time is truly the only resource that cannot. Thus, how the founders and board of directors decide to invest that time and in search of what type of resources is a critical decision.

Tough Question Six: Are You Prepared for the Capital Hunt to Become a Full-Time Occupation?

The capital hunt is often regarded as a side-line or part-time occupation or project, particularly once a company is in the throes of rapid growth. Contrary to this commonly held belief, the capital hunt for most organizations is a full-time occupation for one or more key players in any organization deciding to go this route. And once the hunt begins, it truly never ends!

The philosophy of the founders, the board members they select and to whom they turn for valuable input, and the key players who will be added throughout the course of corporate growth will determine the route the company will select. Strategies that are at odds with one another are more typical than not.

As many an entrepreneur has learned the hard way, early rounds of "unsophisticated" funding or *bootstrapping* techniques do not always please later "sophisticated" players. Often relationships, both investment and operational, established in the early days of the organization will undergo severe alteration to entice the larger investment banking support.

Bootstrappers use whatever means are at their disposal to hold the business together as they seek market penetration, expansion, and increased profit margins in uncommon ways. *Bootstrappers* utilize clever trades, bargain-basement shopping techniques, and strategic alliances to create an enterprise that encompasses characteristics of significantly larger and/or better heeled operations. One example of the ultimate *bootstrapper's* dream is the long-distance telephone services company, ConQuest Telecommunications (ConQuest).

CONQUEST'S GHANSHYAM PATEL

ConQuest founder Ghanshyam Patel came from his native country, India, with just $5 in his pocket. I would love to tell you the story begins there. Sorry. It is a great and true story, but not that far of a stretch. He put his first efforts into learning as much as he could in his chosen field and developing contacts throughout the industry in which he planned to build his dream.

He worked for Sprint and MCI for more than 15 years before launching his own operation. During that time he saved only $4,000. It doesn't seem like much to launch a multimillion-dollar organization. But this is where the story of entrepreneurial endeavor through bootstrapping techniques really begins. With that $4,000, his entrepreneurial skills, and his years of experience inside the industry, he started.

He persuaded a private investor to lend him an additional $25,000. Then he persuaded a bankruptcy judge to let him buy a long-distance carrier that had gone bankrupt to allow him to acquire and service the 400 customers who would now be left in limbo. He made this acquisition for just $5,000.

Next he approached GTE, which held title to the billing equipment of the bankrupt company, worth over $500,000. After doing his research, he determined it would cost GTE $40,000 a year in excise taxes while the equipment sat idle. He convinced GTE to sell it to him for the price of its tax bill plus $1 for the customized software.

He then sold that same equipment to a friend for $250,000 and leased it back in exchange for ConQuest stock. The friend received the benefit of half-price on the equipment, depreciation, plus a percentage of participation in Patel's company.

To acquire the telephone switching system he needed, which went for nearly $3 million in the open market, he went to Northern Telecom. Once again his research (and his old contacts) paid off and he found Northern Telecom had a switch that had been sold to a Detroit company that had also gone bankrupt. He negotiated a price of $500,000, a nothing-down five-year contract, refurbished the system himself, and was in business.

Today ConQuest has 30,000 pay phones and 200 employees. It is likely you utilize the services of ConQuest whether you are aware of it or not. ConQuest is the provider of long-distance service for over 150,000 hospitality rooms in hotels across America.

The best business owners and entrepreneurs who determine that the route for them is OPM put their efforts and time into finding the very best investing partners whose capital and other resources can effectively capture and expand the market for their wares. While you may think all money looks, feels, and smells the same, it doesn't play out that way. The right quality of money is as important as or more important than the quantity of it.

You, as an entrepreneur, have ideas both unique and doable. You have the capacity to assemble a team that can bring the concepts to life. You have the ability to mastermind a plan to create a successful enterprise.

You understand the marketing requirements, profit-margin targets, and existing and potential customer base. You have nearly everything except . . . money! And you may not clearly understand the relationship between that money and the surprises you are likely to encounter in the five major areas of business risk.

Untimely surprises can and will come in one or more of these areas, often more than once. Such surprises face all business enterprises, whether start-ups, mergers, or corporate acquisitions, or in the creation of new divisions. These five areas are business development, manufacturing, marketing, management, and growth. Simple enough.

Not so simple are the strategies and complexity of options available, from a capital perspective, is in dealing successfully with the risks in each and overcoming them. In the next chapter we will look closely at these risks, help you avoid the pitfalls, and hurdle over risk to achieve continued success.

CHAPTER 2

Understanding the Risks of Launching and Funding the Business

Young companies can shoot themselves in the foot very early in their development by simply choosing the inappropriate structure for bringing in the initial rounds of investor monies. Often it is very difficult to convey to entrepreneurs the critical decisions they have to make in the early stages of their development. Either they do it right, or they risk planting the seeds of demise, difficulty, and failure.

Bruce Winkler

President
Prototype Design Systems
(Madison, Wisconsin)

Are *you* ready, really ready to launch or grow your business to its full potential? When you truly are, the investors will be there, should you decide to pursue them.

As you are growing your business, you will have the option to accept outside funding more than once. At any phase in the progress of your organization, you should take the time to fully prepare yourself for the risks inherent in the business before accepting any outside funding.

Answering the following critical questions can help determine your readiness to launch and grow your business. Once you've answered the questions, I suggest you go through the process again with your most important teammates.

The more precisely you understand the risks that pertain to your particular business, their relative import to the investment community, and how to weigh them, the better prepared you will be to address potential investors successfully. Perhaps more important, by preparing yourself for the onslaught of investor questions and barbs, you will be in a far better position to sustain your successful business growth.

To help you understand the tiers of risk more completely, I ask you to think about beginning your business as if you are on the shore and must swim to the island of your dreams. That island on the horizon is the successful business you see in your mind's eye.

The first, and most important, levels of risk to determine are those that define for you the quality and appeal of the island. You must do your reconnaissance to determine just how tantalizing, lush, and sustainable life on that island can be. In other words, you must first determine if it is worth the effort to even attempt the journey.

To get to your island, you must successfully swim across a body of churning, not placid, water. The questions of how long it will take you and whether you will have the stamina to make it are important questions. Are you prepared for a difficult and tiring journey? Be sure it is worthy of the effort.

Will your sponsors encourage and support or distract and abuse you while you make your attempt? Will they lose heart if you are slow in getting to the goal? Will they stick around should you go off course and get you back on the right path or will they stand idly by and let you sink by yourself?

How will you handle the crashing, sometimes crushing waves, especially those that will test you from the very beginning? The heavy, large waves that face you at the shore may seem the most difficult, but other tests of your courage, your commitment, and your dedication are going to follow.

You will face danger on many fronts, including the possibility of shark-infested waters. You may, and probably will, be hit with squalls. You may get close to shore and be torpedoed by cruising pirate ships. None of this fantasy image is all that dissimilar from the journey you are about to take to propel your dream and desire from a mere idea into a sparkling new business.

We will look at risk from this perspective. Examining a series of six major risks will determine the worthiness of the island for you and your potential investors. Understanding these six parameters will help you decide if the idea can and should be borne.

If these can be successfully answered, then the risks that follow will be much like the waves, the pests and creatures, the unexpected weather, and unfriendly forces you may encounter. You will quickly learn they will constantly come your way throughout your journey. Risk has a way of doing that. It just keeps showing up, sometimes when you least expect or want it.

THE SIX MAJOR RISKS OF LAUNCHING
THE BUSINESS

Can You Successfully Grow Your Idea
Into A Business?

The emphasis in this question is twofold. First, is there really a business in your idea? Second, are you the one to make it happen?

An idea that is worth spending time and money to develop is one that has possibilities or probabilities for providing a solution for a major, easily discernible problem that affects a wide audience.

Thus, the problem itself is not the same as the business. The problem sets the stage for the business to be developed. Whatever business you chose to be in is related to some problem, perceived or real, large or small.

Big problems, those that are of a global nature, warrant considerably more attention than small, esoteric problems. Big problems are always addressed by a wide variety of possible solutions (or companies).

If there is no real problem, no matter the inventiveness of the solution or the skill of the management team, little if any serious revenue will be generated. The size of the problem sets the parameters for the possible rewards to be shared in the event of success.

Sophisticated investors, including venture capitalists, rarely get their serious interest tweaked by anything less than ideas that have the potential to become hundred million dollar companies. But they do look at many with substantially smaller market potentials as well. They just want to know it is a sustainable business; it has unique qualities that will attract customers; and the market is large enough to create handsome profits for everyone participating.

Fortunately for you, there are virtually no problems of the most serious magnitude that have perfect solutions to be precisely executed by an ideal team. While you are unlikely to know what any particular source exactly expects in the way of the problem's magnitude and your team's ability to deal with it, you should figure you must be in the top 10 to 20 percent of all contenders attempting to create solutions in your chosen field to get the investment nod.

If you have not done so before, you should research one or more problem index sources to determine the magnitude of the problem you are setting out to tackle. Two leading sources to investigate are the *New York Times* and the *Washington Post*. Both share on a daily basis the problems being faced around the globe in the physical, social, and industrial spheres.

John Naisbitt, author of *Megatrends,* has a firm that tracks lines of print devoted to various topics in local, regional, and national newspapers. This is his methodology of spotting major concerns of people. Another method to determine highly rated problems is to analyze how much is being expended to research given problems on an annual basis. Then figure out who is spending it.

The more people (individuals and institutions) willing to pay for solutions, the higher the price to get them. The higher the price for the solution, the higher the potential rewards for the risk takers.

Faith Popcorn, author of *The Popcorn Report,* researches in a similar fashion to Naisbitt to forecast the future trends of society. Beyond this, she created BrainReserve over 20 years ago. This brain trust of people of good minds from many disciplines shares observations about what is happening and what trends are developing.

Out of Popcorn's BrainReserve she created a TalentBank that today has over 2,000 members and is widely hailed as one of the leading expert talent and mind banks in existence. Her now widely recognized and discussed "cocoon" syndrome was first spotted and forecast in the late 1970s. The number of highly successful ventures that are party to this particular trend is already legendary.

Trends, even bigger than a single problem, do not end. They evolve. Correctly forecasting the majority reactions (trends) to widespread problems is perhaps risky business but it also opens up a more comprehensive view of the problem(s) to be dealt with.

Some of the *big* problems of our society today include:

Aging.

Chemical abuse.

Communication.

Computer literacy.

Crime.

Disease and disability.

Environment.

Government cost and effectiveness

Health care, traditional and holistic.

Hunger.

Self-esteem.

Survival of the fittest.

Let's say you have passed the first checkpoint. The idea is a good one that can sustain a business being developed around it. Now, what will it take to develop the idea into a working solution? Can it be done at a reasonable cost, in a timely manner, and with significant profit margins?

The solution has two major ingredients, the technology and the plan to deliver the solution to the problem. If both are strong, the solution will get high ratings. It will take a good, if not great, team to make the best idea pan out and turn into a profitable business. In fact, as has been said, and I am among those who say it, "A good idea with the wrong or weak people will never get off the ground. A mediocre or even poor idea with great people will."

The time and initial capital risk to determine just how good your idea is and what its potential can be are your expense—your contribution. The investment of your time to fully develop the idea is your greatest risk *and,* eventually, your greatest asset. This is why the reality check is so important. Getting outside investors to participate at this totally unproven stage is wishful thinking or even foolish.

Is Your Solution Feasible?

If the solution is a product, it should be proprietary. If it is a service, its delivery system should be unable to be duplicated. If not that, it must have a penetration and a lead time that will be tremendously expensive to duplicate or even compete with.

Patents, process patents, and lead time are the most important aspects of proprietary product to serious capital sources. If you have none of these, you may have little to offer. The truism is, "If you have something worth doing, it will be worth duplicating." It is only a matter of time.

Natural monopolies do not last long without government protection. If you have no protection for the product you have developed, the delivery system for it must truly shine. Either it should be virtually incapable of being copied or be prohibitively expensive, thus creating a barrier to entry from competition.

To provide an *elegant* solution to a given problem, you must have an incisive means of delivering something profound to address the problem. *Elegant* connotes something done with style, with class. In other words, you blow away the competition. Your answer is at once both simple and profound. This is the solution you wish to represent.

To deliver in this fashion, you need to determine what it will take in terms of time, people, capital, and other resources. It is at this stage of macro risk taking that you may be able to lure investors. While this level of risk playing is still highly susceptible to failure, some investors are willing to play at this level.

As for capital participation from outside parties, this phase is rarely funded by sophisticated *angels* (private funding sources) or venture capital groups. In this phase entrepreneurs usually apply their bootstrapping methods or begin the search for OPM. When the latter is involved, the source is often close to home.

Friends, family, wealthy individuals known personally by the entrepreneur, and suppliers familiar with the entrepreneur are the best bet to invest at this stage. This is, as you can easily surmise, the highest risk time for all projects and organizations.

Sophisticated investors, when secured at this juncture, demand much, much more than those sources known personally to the founder. During this and the next phase of risk, there is no positive cash flow on which an investor can rely. Thus, they will and do demand greater equity participation. Their anticipation is to cash in the chips later for a *very significant* multiple on their dollars.

Thus, a more realistic view of funding at this level is to expect to do so with your own time and money. Your capacity to string together the resources you need without outside financing will be taken by investors you approach later as a sign of commitment and accomplishment. It also allows you to grow the company to a less risky level without complicating the picture too much with outside equity participation.

The important thing for all entrepreneurs and intrapreneurs to remember is that it is the *implementation* of breakthrough ideas, not necessarily the ideas themselves, that separates the amateurs from the professionals. Investors are well aware of this. At this stage of the game, implementation has yet to be proven.

This stage of your business development, when expressed as a level of risk, is commonly termed *seed* capital despite all the effort you may have put into your thinking, researching, and assembling your own dream team. Capital will be spent at this level to determine the viability of the business. The symbolism is appropriate.

It is from seeds that tall oaks grow. Small flowers grow from seeds, too. Thinking about it in these terms, you can quickly understand the differences in the amount of nourishment (resources) and the required frequency (rounds of possible financing) that will be needed.

Knowing from the beginning if you are planting a sunflower or a tall oak, you will make better decisions regarding the timing and amount of resources required for the planting to reach maturity.

Of course, weeds grow from seeds as well. Beware the misdirection of resources so that the weeds do not grow too numerous, too quickly and ultimately choke out the life of your endeavors.

To determine what you are planting, be it weed, sunflower, or oak tree, get realistic about the potential of the market for the product or service you are creating. Then, do your homework to assess whether or not it can be feasibly produced and sold at a profitable enough margin to warrant its existence.

Doing your homework on these first two steps of the *big* risk picture will go a long way in determining the extent of resources you will ultimately require.

Can You Get It Produced?

You know it is feasible. You know how much it is going to cost to develop the goods or services. You have identified the various resources and people needed to make it happen. Now, can you actually get it done (produced)?

Setting up the manufacturing can be a tedious process or it can be a simple matter. The key elements to the decision process are the cost of production, the timeliness of delivery to the customer, and, ultimately, the distinct advantage provided by your product or delivery of service to the customer.

Sophisticated investors still shy away from participation at this phase of the corporate development because the factors that directly affect successful production are normally not in their control. Whether or not the product (or the delivery/distribution system for the service you intend to provide) can be produced at a price significantly competitive for customers to jump ship from their current suppliers is one major factor. Only the customers can answer whether or not they will.

Another factor to be considered at this phase is whether the goods can be produced at a price enticing enough for the potential customers to decide to solve a problem they have learned to live with. Far too often, entrepreneurs overlook this very real fact of life about getting people to change, even when their current situation is painful or ineffective.

The only answer to absolving the risk at this level is to have an *unfair advantage* over the competition. In a service organization, this is a delivery system that is extremely difficult to duplicate in either a short time or at a low cost. In a product-oriented organization, it is to have an absolutely bullet-proof, worldwide patented, proprietary product. If you have neither of those, then you fall into the great melting pot with the other 90 to 95 percent of businesses.

Thus, the risk the potential investors face is still quite high. Without proprietary advantages, your business is faced with creating niche advantages that are not nearly so distinct or recognizable.

Will Anyone Buy It?

So you can make it. You can even make it at a very attractive and competitive price. The question is, Will anyone buy it? And will enough buy it to make it a sustainable enterprise?

At this point serious, sophisticated investors enter the picture for those organizations that have successfully passed through the first three phases of risk. Having tested your price point and market acceptance and established a viable product or service that customers may want, you are now in a position to take on the risk of marketing the product.

This is where venture capitalist or corporate partners can be especially effective. Not only will their money propel the growth of the organization, but also their contacts and abilities to successfully extract the maximum benefit from the dollars expended can propel you like a rocket.

A good homework assignment at this point is to ask those potential customers yourself *before* you produce it. This will allow you to determine whether this fabulous product or service will actually entice any customers.

This is what alpha and beta site testing is all about. The best way to determine whether your assumptions are right about the level of demand for your goods is to ask real customers. Of course, you should not expect your competitors to sit idly by while you scoop their customers out from underneath their noses. Expect and plan for their competitive response. Always think out at least two or three steps into the future.

Will Existing Management Be Capable of Changing from Entrepreneurial Launch to Sustained Growth?

You've done it. You have launched a successful business, with products and/or services well received in the market, produced at a reasonable cost and in a timely fashion, and market demand promises to continue to grow.

What other risks could there be? From this stage on, that risk falls clearly into the category of management. The risks of getting anything started are considerably different from the risks in keeping something alive.

Can your existing management team actually make money consistently? Both elements of that are important—making money and doing it consistently. That is, after all, the key to continued success.

If the type of manager you have attracted at the initiation of the organization is a far cry from the type you will need once operating on a more or less even keel, you must prepare for the changing of the guard. This is one of the most critical elements to your business capitalization because it is critical to your business survival.

Energy Is the Fuel Required to Run a Successful Company!

Implementing a plan and a strategy well takes energy. All team members need it, and the leader most of all. Long hours and six- or seven-day weeks are more the norm than not in leading companies. This is true whether in their initial phase or in their expansion mode. That means management members need to be healthy. Only when they are healthy can they derive the energy required to stand up to the rigorous physical and emotional demands of building successful projects and companies.

Energy, along with attitude, is one of those qualities that can be incredibly contagious. Excitement and energy have a tremendous tendency to build on one another, creating an environment ripe for creative development. This is truly one hallmark of the entrepreneurial project or company!

Another element of energy, too often overlooked or understated, is the frequent expression in top organizations that, "This is sheer fun." High-energy individuals have a great outlook. The result is they have a great time in life. That gets reflected in the organizations to which they are affiliated.

If investors were to peek in on your group, ask yourself, "Would they be seeing happy, productive, highly energized people some, most, or none of the time?" If the answer is anything but most, you have some serious work to do to get your team into gear!

A History of Achievement Portends a Future of the Same!

Individually and collectively, the management teams of high-performance companies have a history of achievement. Achievement throughout a lifetime of experience is one of the best indicators of achievement in the future.

I have read that the best correlation between past achievement and current entrepreneurial success is that of the Eagle Scout. The point being: Achievement begins at an early age and continues throughout achievers' lives.

Teams That Exemplify Honesty and Integrity Win!

The management teams of the most successful companies are always composed of individuals of high integrity who are at times excruciatingly honest. Rather than try to gloss over holes in the idea, organization, or fulfillment of the organization's goals, team players on high performance teams are honest about what is and is not working. Rather than try to shore up their own self-importance or performance, their emphasis is on making things work.

Management members of this caliber are seeking solutions to problems, not hiding from them. Honesty, whether with the customer, the employees, or the investors is not an option. Working with this guideline, such management teams cannot tolerate operating, production, sales, or service practices based on esoteric or personal agendas that conflict with the greater good of the whole.

Integrity is all too often something easy to talk about (and is!) in the world today; it is quite another to see it acted out in day-to-day operations. Companies that exude integrity from top to bottom stand out to virtually everyone. It is not always easy to be a leader striving to operate profitably while maintaining personal and ethical methods and values. The best companies do!

Resourcefulness Leads to Trying on New Ideas and Embarking on New Paths

Expansive growth never comes about in an orderly, preconceived pattern. While doing your best to plan for all critical moves to take your organization to fulfillment of its goals, things can and will go awry. The twists and turns, ups and downs of organizations growing and changing to meet the demands of an ever-changing marketplace are just part of the game.

To operate in such an environment of chaos requires a highly effective team. It takes clear focus and the ability to size up situations quickly, communicate internally and externally with the proper parties, and respond effectively to situations on demand in order to utilize all resources within each member's grasp.

Creativity and inquisitiveness, coupled with an open mind, are critical to achieve the high level of resourcefulness required to be the best.

Problems come when they are often least expected or appreciated. To turn these lemons into lemonade, extraordinarily resourceful, lateral thinking is required.

Digging deep to find solutions that break the mold can take an inordinate amount of courage. It also means revising your way of thinking about a problem or an opportunity. Such thinking then leads to actions that may be uncomfortable because they are out of the norm of prior behavior. This is what resourceful management teams do time and time again. In challenging themselves to stretch and grow, they open up previously untapped resources to assist them.

Pro Teams Maximize Resources by Analyzed Application and a Real Sense of Their Operating Environment

The last area that defines consistently performing management teams is that of succinct analysis and efficient responsiveness. Top managers quickly analyze situations to determine what can and what should be done. They have the ability to get "real" in a hurry. In doing so, they do not hesitate to set aside or leave behind people, plans, products, and the like that are not working.

Like laser beams, top management teams can decide which routes to take to achieve maximum results. They have a clear picture of their goals and what it will take to accomplish them. Rarely do they buy their own hype or get caught up in it. Real facts will determine the outcomes. They are well aware of this and act accordingly.

As in "triage" in the medical profession, top business teams determine in all crisis situations (whether positive or negative) who and what to emphasize and who and what to detach and leave behind. The who are the people involved. The what includes particular business deals, alliances and acquisitions, production or sales decisions, marketing or advertising campaigns,

Great management teams have a strong sense of urgency to get things done—done quickly, efficiently, and profitably. Doing that well takes an understanding of who the key players should be, how well and consistently they perform, and when and how to tell their continued usefulness. Once again, it is the people more than the particular situation facing them that is most crucial to achieve consistent and outstanding performance.

Virtually all critical business decisions made by the people involved in them can be viewed in the same fashion as a physical battle.

There are those players who walk away from skirmishes unscathed and ready to do battle another day. These are the strongest and the luckiest.

There are others who avoid battles. They choose to stay on the sidelines to read the outcomes of critical business "battles" before lending their support one way or another.

Outstanding management teams are well aware of who the consistent players are who walk away as champions. These become their best lieutenants and commanders for future dealings.

There are others on the field of play who suffer varying degrees of harm in the engagement. There are those for whom nothing more can be done; they have suffered irreversible damage that will soon lead to their deaths. In many cases they may already be dead without even knowing it.

There are those who are only superficially wounded. These can get by on their own to get help from supporting forces. They do not require a great deal of time and energy to enhance their recovery.

Great management recognizes its players who leave a particular battlefield mortally wounded, but who have considerable life left in them. These are the ones that get their full attention. Without that focus, they may be lost. With it, they will return to do battle another day. Using resources wisely to maximum benefit where it most counts is the hallmark of these crack teams.

For everyone with an idea, it is great fun to see that idea launched and working. For everyone concerned, founders, investors, employees, suppliers, and even to some extent customers, it is imperative to survival that the idea gets to and sustains profitability.

Once you achieve the plateau of business as usual, steady, slowing in the rate of growth, or sustaining an existing client base, you are likely to encounter serious turnover of the original entrepreneurial team. At what often appears to be the first blush of success, shifts in outlook and decision making are required to take the organization from start-up into maturity. Many entrepreneurs and entrepreneurial management teams bail at this juncture. Their thrill is in the chase, not in the long-term management of success.

You might think of the process much like the maturation of children. The requirement in the early years is in acquiring the necessary skills to survive. Once past that challenge and excitement of survival, new skills and outlook are needed to move into maturity. The same is true for your company.

Because this is reality for the vast majority of companies, the risk to be discussed in the earliest phases of your capital hunt is that of finding your replacements, only better (from a managerial point of view). Again, investors often are your best source of candidates. The investors at this level like the fact that the serious incline of the risk is behind the business now. This is a playing field they feel is far more advantageous because it is much flatter, with relatively minor hills and bumps to contend with in the future.

Can the Business Sustain Explosive Growth?

Can you and your organization shift into high gear and manage extraordinary growth successfully? How long do you expect to sustain a high (greater than 50 percent annual) growth rate? What happens then?

The dream of everyone in your entire organization, before you even begin with the first step of actualization, is to have unending, explosive growth that will be met by untethered, explosive reward. The reality is that such a scenario is a fantasy (with only a handful of exceptions, including IBM and Microsoft).

One of the most difficult challenges many successful young companies face is to handle explosive growth rates year to year beyond a period of three or four years. Extraordinary success can be every bit as dangerous as imminent failure.

In these first three to five years of extraordinary high growth, the risks you and the entire team, investors included, will be willing to take will far outstrip the risks you will be prepared to take once you begin a plateauing of growth. In the early years, for the company and for the entrepreneurial founding team, you have little to risk and everything to gain by taking leaps into unproven territory.

Once you build up the asset base in terms of reputation, name, and capital evaluation, your willingness to risk diminishes immensely. When you are risking the company and it isn't worth much, it is so much easier.

At this risk level most companies are ready for a new set of investing partners to continue their existence and slower growth. Venture capitalists are ready to get off the ride at this juncture, and friends and family are normally ready to cash in their chips as well.

You and the team, in fact, are usually ready to participate in some long-awaited financial rewards, too. This, then, is the most appropriate time to enter into the arena of public investors.

Once your business reaches a level of maturity, with sustained existence and profitability, future growth will go through the same six levels of risk we have just outlined. The introduction of new products and new services will take the same route the parent company has undergone. Each must go through a determination of the viability of the idea, its feasibility, the probability of effective production, how well and quickly it will gain market acceptance and demand, how long effective management can sustain a growth cycle for the product or service, and at what level does it get spun off, bought out, or merged in some fashion.

The spin-off of new divisions, joint ventures, or mergers will all require an effective and collaborative effort to achieve investor funding while maintaining the value structure and integrity of the parent organization. For companies that live long lives, these risk levels are repeated numerous times as new products, services, distribution networks, marketing approaches, and management teams turn over.

If you can clearly pass the hurdle of the major risks to doing the business that we have just outlined, you are ready. Now you are going to face the pesky risks that will repeatedly affect the business from inception through growth.

THE RISKS IN GROWING THE BUSINESS

To get started with these detailed risks, understand they are the second tier of decision making. Once we have reviewed them, you may want to list the most significant risks in each category that you anticipate in completion of your own 30-day, 60-day, first-year, and second-year goals.

The peskiest risks include the following:

Financial

- Can you find or create sufficient capital to get through the first and probably the second level of risk for the business (viability and feasibility)?
- Can you find sufficient capital whenever you need it to sustain or grow the business?
- What happens if you don't have sufficient capital at a critical point?
- Do you overcapitalize in anticipation of problems or to provide for contingencies? Can you afford to do this?

- How quickly will you create income? Become profitable?
- How will you establish cash flow (not the same as income) on a consistent and timely basis?
- How are you providing for contingencies that cost money (i.e., slow sales, unanticipated cost overruns, being dead wrong on market acceptance, price point, competition, taxes, and licenses)?
- When can you reasonably expect to return any cash to investors?
- What are the major financial risks the company will sustain in development, production, distribution, and sales?

Personnel

- Do you have A, B, or C people on your management team?
- When and how many A people do you need? Can you afford?
- What criteria are you using to measure the team members?
- How can you entice A people when you don't have the capital to pay them what they want and deserve and all you can afford are C players?
- Where will you find the best players if you don't have them?
- How many hats can one person wear? How long?
- What will make the core team stick around through the most crucial rounds of development?
- In what order will you add critical players?
- How will you juggle compensation with tight budgeting?
- Can you acquire good people through acquisition?
- Are core values or expertise most important to you?
- Are you creating a corporate culture? Inheriting one that may or may not be ascribed to your core members? Leaving its creation up to chance?

Design and Development

- Is the design and/or development proprietary?
- Can it be patented? Copyrighted? Trademarked?
- What amount of lead time do you have on the competition?
- How will you defend patent infringement or copycats?

- How many ways can you come up with to accomplish the same goal?
- What other disciplines might offer guidance or solutions to your design and development dilemmas?

Manufacturing and Production

- What criteria and priority are being used to determine in-house versus outside manufacturing?
- Is time to delivery or price more important to the customer base you are developing?
- What other criteria of manufacturing/production are important to your customers, salespeople, corporate image? Quality? Pricing? Service? Reliability? Consistency? Innovation? Longevity? Accessibility?
- What financial factors will affect location, equipment, personnel and equipment utilization, and delivery?

Marketing and Advertising

- How will you measure the effectiveness of the marketing campaign? Its components?
- Who will determine the objectives of marketing campaigns for the business and the various products and divisions?
- Are there effective means of reaching the same or a larger customer base by means other than those being employed?
- How can you creatively bootstrap or barter for more effective use of funds in the business?
- What lateral thoughts does the team have in drawing from their past experiences, current research, or other industries?
- How will you test the various means of advertising for results? Compared to what?
- How do you differentiate between short-term ad campaigns and long-term name recognition ones?
- Are you effectively using sponsorship and nonprofit organizational support to enhance your image?

Distribution and Sales

- Should you stay in-house or outsource distribution? Sales?
- Can you manage multiple levels of distribution?
- Does the sales team get revved up before the product is ready or does the product get ready before you sign on the dynamic sales force?
- How do you provide incentives that are meaningful with your type of product/service?
- Who makes the best type of sales team for your unique product/service?
- What will be your response to slipping sales? Nonexistent sales? Higher than anticipated sales?
- How will you balance the demands from the sales team against those of the production team?
- Can you effectively manage both in-house sales with outsourced distribution without ruffling feathers?
- When and how do you need to boost sales? When and how do you need to keep them stable? When and how do you need to keep them quieted?
- What are the critical factors for you in the distribution channels selected? How, when, and why will they alter?

Customers, Customers, Customers

- Are you sure you will have enough?
- Will the customers buy at a price you can afford to produce and deliver?
- How can you build customer loyalty to your product/service?
- How important will servicing be to retain your customers?
- How can you "up-sell" the customers? Do you have anything else to offer to do it with?
- Of the key factors about your product or service, can you determine what is important in any sort of priority ranking? How? Are you capable of monitoring and tracking sales?
- Are there geographical, gender, age, cultural differences important to understand about your customer base?

- How can you enhance sales to markets outside the targets your team initially sets?
- How will you respond to declining customer interest?
- Can you grow the market for the product? How?
- What steps can you take from the very beginning of product/ service introduction to build in customer satisfaction, referral, and repeat purchase?

In all categories, these are just some of the questions you and your team, as well as the investors who fund you, should be asking. It gets you started by putting you in the shoes of those whose assistance you seek to make your business successful.

(Remember, as you begin this process, that you are looking into the near-term future. This is just the beginning. Looking further into the longer-term future gets cloudier but is still an interesting and valuable process.)

Before we complete this discussion of the risk both you and the potential investors are about to take, let's look at risk through the often "unspoken" veil that affects the risk you will all take. That veil is composed of the personal values you bring to owning and operating the business.

First, let's review the risks to doing business that must be addressed before any business can be effectively launched or expanded:

Is the idea viable enough to grow into a business?

Is the fulfillment of the idea feasible from a cost, time, and profit perspective?

Can the product or service be produced effectively?

Is there a sustainable market for it?

Can sustained profitability be managed?

Once explosive growth tapers off, what's next to keep the business alive and well?

The constant areas of risk that will pummel you time and time again include:

Financial risks.

Personnel risks.

Product design and development risks.

Manufacturing and production risks.

Marketing and advertising risks.

Sales and distribution risks.

Customer risks.

Now, to lift the veil through which you see the world, let's look at the values you personally believe in and those you employ in your business life.

A partial list of values you might choose from are these:

Commitment	Confidence
Responsibility	Risk tolerant and taking
Energy	Excellence
Action-oriented	Accomplishment-oriented
Truth	Teamwork
Elegant	Empowering
Innovation	Intelligence
Networking	Novelty
Drive	Determination
Integrity	Incorruptible
Visionary	Vital
Ideals	Imagination
Desire	Daring
Understanding	Unique
Artful	Awesome
Love	Life
Goal setting	Growth-oriented
Outgoing	Optimistic
Attitude	Altruistic
Leadership	Learning
Self-confident	Self-esteem

From this list or others, list the 10 most important values by which you live your life. (The above list compiles the most qualities consistently demonstrated by successful entrepreneurs.) Once listed, prioritize your selections. Now, analyzing the list carefully, determine (1) how many of them you are employing in your business and planning and (2) the five key values you most consistently demonstrate personally in the operation of your business. Whatever those values may be, they will be the ones reflected throughout the operation and will become the root of the corporate culture you are building.

At this point, you may learn some invaluable insights. *It is common to hold different values and priorities in our business lives than in our personal ones. It will be the degree to which the two are out of sync that will cause conflict in your life.*

With this personal information now brought back to the front of your consciousness, it is up to you to determine what is acceptable or nonacceptable risk in launching and funding this business. Of the many risks we have outlined, your response to addressing and then solving them should be made in a way that is congruent with your personal value system.

THE RISKS OF FUNDING THE BUSINESS

You have assessed the risk of whether or not it is a good idea to even begin the business. You have determined the answers to all major areas you can foresee might create heartache and grief. And you still want to bring in OPM to make it all happen.

To help you understand a bit more clearly what you are about to undertake, let's look at risk through the eyes of the potential investor. Then we will look at the risk of accepting their investment participation from the perspective of how you will structure it to maximize the benefit for *both* sides.

Risk Seen Through the Eyes of the Investor (or the Better You "See" Through Their Eyes, the Better Your Chance of Funding)

How investors will look at the risk you are offering them is considerably different from how you and your team look at it. One way sophisticated investors use is outlined below.

It is important for you to understand where you are coming from in assessing risk and where they begin in assessing risk for themselves. You may have the opportunity to share your own assessment with them in longer presentations, but you can do so only if you have gone through the personal exercise we just described.

Investors tend to see risk only in terms of the return of their principal and how much they will make on the investment. One formula to accomplish this is:

$$O \times R \times V = D$$

O = Opportunity (weighted most heavily)
R = Resources required to achieve success
V = Value they judge is provided by the product/service
D = Investment decision on a personal priority scale

In dealing with potential investors, you might wish to apply this formula to both your thinking and the eventual presentation of your unique offering. Determine in your own mind what you see as the opportunity (the size and richness of the island), the resources and their cost needed to bring it to life (money, team, facilities, distribution, marketing), and the value you will be creating for the targeted market (the vision and mission of the business).

By answering those first six business levels of risk we started with at the beginning of this chapter, you will be ready for bear. By answering the risk questions for yourself before you are asked to answer them for potential investors, you are two or more steps ahead of them. Your preparation will pay off with both the capital you seek and with better preparation to handle whatever comes your way in growing the business.

Another question to ask yourself in preparation for addressing the risk concerns of the potential investors is whether your expectations are realistic about the timing and the makeup of possible investment capital.

The old adage that "It will take longer and cost more" is more often the case than not. Some risks are directly linked to capital funding or utilization, others only indirectly or subtly. This is your opportunity to think through the relationship so as to be better prepared at every turn. And that is the object of the game.

Suggestion: Using the lists you created above, estimate the potential costs involved with every risk outlined. This will give you a clearer picture of your possible need for funds as you proceed. It will also help you define alternative solutions with greater ease.

By completing this step in the early stages, you will be better prepared to determine the potential timing of future rounds of financing, as well as the particular method or structuring that will be most effective at that time. This leads us to the risks of funding the business in terms of type of funding, timing of funding, and the structure by which funds are accepted.

The Risks of Structure

Something that affects you at least as much as who the potential investors are is how the offering will be structured. If you structure in the wrong way you may be risking the bank, without even knowing it. In Chapter 5 we will go into structuring in depth, but here I want to alert you to some risks inherent in different choices.

Capital structuring can be simple, or complex, depending on the various types and the timing of your particular requirements.

Structural choices should be made on the basis of several different components. In the investor's mind, the burning question is always the relationship between the risk of his or her capital and the potential reward of what *you* are bringing to the table. How you see it and how the investor sees it are two entirely different perspectives.

Your assessment of the risk for you and the organization should focus on the relationship between the cost of the capital and its timeliness and necessity to the growth of the enterprise. By understanding risk as investors see it and responding to their spoken and unspoken concerns, you will establish clearer, more realistic expectations on both parts. This will allow you to create working relationships that can weather the storms you are likely to encounter between inception and ultimate payoff.

Structurally speaking, all choices revolve around two basic forms of capital infusion, debt or equity. Debt is simply borrowed money, usually collateralized with some form of asset. *Because debt will become a drain on the corporate cash flow, utilizing the funds in a manner that will allow for its earliest and least costly retirement is one major objective to consider.* Equity is contributed capital evidenced by ownership in either the entire operation or some specific component of it.

While most entrepreneurs almost automatically fund their needs through equity, that financing route has been the ruin of many. *By selling too much equity too soon, the founders can find themselves holding little equity for their hard work.* Without regard for the alternatives available or by failing to heed the needs the company is sure to have for future rounds of financing, equity can often seem the expeditious answer to the entrepreneur hungry for building his or her business venture.

Considering the actual application of the funds should be a primary determinant for the type of funding you select. Then choosing the particular structure can be customized to the unique requirements of your organization at any given time.

As there are only six major ways in which capital will be utilized within the organization, coordinating the type of funding that works most appropriately for each is, at least in theory, a relatively simple matter. Interestingly, more often than not start-up companies do not heed this guideline. In all likelihood it is because they have not learned it or their common sense has been overruled in the face of expedience.

Debt works best for capital equipment expenditures, short-term working capital needs for inventory, accounts receivable expansion, and project-specific marketing and advertising expenses. It may also prove to be your best choice in selected acquisitions. *When the company being acquired has assets that lend themselves to near-term liquidation or significant cash flow generation, acquiring such assets with debt is the best alternative.*

Equity funding works best for seed capital needs, long-term marketing and advertising costs that are part of building a corporate image and name, operating working capital (remember to keep that belt tight, especially at the beginning), manufacturing, and distribution channel buildup. It also works well for acquisitions that involve significant but illiquid assets.

Combinations of debt and equity work well for companies with multiple needs when the total amount of funds required is fairly evenly balanced. Such combination also is the most effective for organizations that can time their capital needs in a well-prepared program.

The care and feeding of the company is much better accomplished when the officers and managers focus on the business elements to create growth rather than juggling with cash flow problems.

Debt/equity structuring should be used as a tool by astute business owners and their financial officers during the early to intermediate stages of growth. The risks of losing control and giving up too much equity can be ameliorized with this strategy.

Situations that call for a debt-to-equity conversion are the best solution for those corporate or project leaders who need capital immediately, but do not yet have a fully thought through plan. Again, risk is reduced because of a simple structural strategy.

Convertible solutions also work well in uncertain times of corporate expansion, when the full picture of end results may be somewhat fuzzy. Determining a feasible conversion ratio based on forecasts may be less formidable for the founders, and the potential investors are likely to be less demanding as well.

As long as the company can afford the cash required to meet the interest payments, this solution allows the owners to retain more of the corporate stock and ensure equity participation as they meet the milestones of corporate growth and perform according to plan. It also satisfies the "feel good" aspect investors like by getting even modest cash return into their hands relatively early.

Deciding on the proper structuring for your particular endeavor or enterprise is not all that complex or complicated. The decision-making process is actually quite simple—once you understand the parameters regarding the type of investment you will seek at each level and how best to choose it. Then you are on your own. Only you can apply these structural choices in a manner consistent with your own corporate philosophy.

In Chapter 5, we will go into further detail on application of type, timing, and the legal forms of structuring your company. The most important thing to remember regarding risk from this funding structural view is that you are in control. You and your advisors decide the structure in virtually all cases. In all my experience, I have rarely seen investors promote the structure by which they will invest. Thus, you can be in the driver's seat on this issue.

Keep in mind that whenever, from beginning to end, the business can do without outside funding, you will have much greater flexibility in the capital-raising process. Your risk of losing control or not getting paid well for your efforts is remarkably reduced.

Remember these simple axioms:

- Ownership at any level is easy to give away, mighty hard to recoup.
- The original pie can only be split into 100 percent.
  After that you must make lots of little pies,
  like dangling participles from the parent, or begin
  an entirely new pie.

CHAPTER 3

Building Credibility by Building a Business Plan That Clearly Represents Your Business

There are business plans and there are business plans. Many entrepreneurs and company founders have a lot of difficulty writing business plans. You need to pour your passion into that plan . . . tell the world about that burning idea, innovation, invention you have that will transform systems and touch lives. If you can't write even the draft of a business plan, maybe you better rethink starting a new company. Building a company requires stamina, vision, robust health, and great persistence!

Robert Gold
Chief executive officer
CyberKnight International Corporation
(Austin, Texas)

Business plans can be as succinct as one written on the back of a napkin or as voluminous as a book. Either is fine as long as it accurately represents the who, what, when, why, and how of accomplishing what you are setting out to do.

Business plans are the living, breathing operating manuals by which those enterprises that ultimately succeed operate. Sooner or later those enterprises launched and operating without any idea of where they are headed or how they have accomplished what they have will ultimately fail.

To operate with consistency and ultimate effectiveness either individually or as part of any organization, the decisions made and actions taken must be done in a state of consciousness and with some level of competency.

Business plans are as unique as their creators. They can be used to accomplish one or multiple purposes. The business plan is merely a tool. How it is used is at the discretion of those privy to its contents and purpose.

Business plans are often created to accomplish a variety of chores. The primary reason is to raise money for the entrepreneurial business. But well-conceived and -written business plans can simultaneously serve a variety of critical functions.

The business plan can be used as a marketing and/or educational aid in building or expanding your business, thus allowing for the consistent, successful operation of your venture. Writing the business plan from the perspective of the "life" of the entity to which you have given birth can also help you effectively leave the organization. Exit strategies are important and too often overlooked. How, when, and why you (either personally or the entire corporation) get out of the business can be planned for in an orderly fashion—if you prepare for it in the plan.

The business plan is an ever-changing and vitally important manual designed by the founders and their advisors. It needs to be constantly tweaked and altered if it is to effectively help the business grow. Without frequent updating and input it cannot consistently be a useful and usable tool in creating meaningful results for your organization, employees, investors, and customers.

Business plans are working plans that require constant feedback and input to keep them functional and effective. The mission and purpose define the reason for being. The business plan defines how to function successfully moment by moment throughout every phase of the process.

GET INPUT FROM KEY PLAYERS

In today's "virtual" world brought to our very doorsteps and desktops through ever-advancing technology, you could have everyone in your organization networked into the business plan. In real time, everyone you designate could (should you choose) be allowed daily review and input.

With the use of networking, interactive, and real-time communications available today, any size organization can share not only its purpose but also the plan to achieve it. While this may have been a bold concept just a decade ago (to say nothing of the almost insurmountable cost and time hurdles for any small to medium-sized operation to achieve it), wise business leaders today are allowing increased interactive participation in building and updating their plans.

To be effective, essential managers and employees need to know far more than the mission or purpose of the enterprise to which they may have attached their star. Mission statements are usually posted proudly for employees, customers, and the world to see. But what of the business plan? Is the business plan something you take off a shelf and dust off every now and then and share only with those designated as the insiders who truly "need to know"? Or does it have a more expansive purpose? I propose the most successful businesses of the new millennium will answer yes to the latter question.

Think of your company's business plan as the road map to get everyone you want and/or need to the destination you have outlined, in the manner you would most like to achieve. If you don't provide critical team members with the map, they are likely to make their decisions in their own way, in their own time.

Remember, you are leader of the pack—not a dictator. You have a precise destination in mind for you and the organization. It is important to get the rest of the pack not so much as following but as enrolled with you. Don't even think about drawing up your road map alone!

It is important that all members know what the destination is, can freely communicate with you and the others when and if shortcuts or obstacles block the original path selected, and know the priority the organization places on time, expense, creativity, and so on. Otherwise, only you may know where you are headed and you may be alone in the pursuit. Or you might lead the pack down bumpy, even dangerous, paths that might otherwise be avoided.

Without clear, constant direction and guidance from you (or the plan), managers may lead their division and/or themselves down paths inconsistent with what you have in mind. Providing managers *and* workers with the plan to accomplish the mission you have jointly set out to accomplish is only logical, if you truly wish their assistance to reach your goals rather than those they may create on their own.

Everyone *you* designate as important, whether they are on board with you from the beginning or you expect to add them later, needs the tenets of the basic plan or map. With the basic guideline in their hands, they can now most effectively help you and themselves by filling in the "meat" of the actual business operations as the business evolves. This is how you can make your plan improve and consistently have the business meet its time, financial, and human commitments as desired.

For too many organizations, frontline knowledge is often not translated into the overall operation until it may be too late. Or such information is considered of little consequence and importance because the worker bees are kept in the dark about what the *real* operating business plan calls for at each step of the plan.

Such exchange of information, concepts, ideas, and alternatives can allow for alteration in course, acceleration of product development, and creative marketing and/or selling strategies to be implemented expeditiously. This invaluable feedback will allow for greater success with greater frequency and consistency. Remember: *The best business plan, no matter the business of the enterprise, is one that allows the managers or operators to operate consciously and competently. Only with both is consistency achieved.*

Those business leaders who fail to heed this underlying principle of existence will ultimately end up in the stack heap of bankruptcies or worse! The vast majority end up in the land of the *walking dead.* I use this term to describe that state of existence somewhere between being vibrant, effective, and demonstrating a high level of consistency in thought and action and the alternative of being buried six feet under.

Unfortunately, this is where a considerable number of businesses actually exist, as do far too many individuals. They are alive . . . barely. Some exist from payroll to payroll. Others somehow secure funding or an extension to keep alive and barely breathing but never accumulate enough resources, cash or otherwise, to get out of the ditch and start moving ahead down the road.

The point is to make your business plan, which in very short order becomes your operating plan, something meaningful for you and the key participants. One that is slipshod, poorly constructed, confusing in its detail or complexity, and misunderstood by the very people who will be expected to utilize it is one that needs further work. It is that simple.

A fair number of businesses are being run partially or even totally unconscious of what, who, when, where, and how to make everything fall into place when it is most desirable. And some of them actually survive, even thrive. But if you want the odds in your favor, take the time and expend the energy to create a business plan that is an accurate reflection of your thoughts on where you want to go and your ideas on how best to get there.

To make your plan effective, you must be *clear, concise, complete, candid, committed, charismatic, conservative, confident, and convincing. When you write the plan with these in mind, you will be credible!*

The components that comprise all plans are quite simple. There are six of them, which we will discuss later in this chapter after a review of the decisions you need to make before putting pen to paper.

The complexity in the plan comes initially in determining which of those six components you should emphasize and under what circumstances. This means you will make more than one version of the business plan.

Businesses get more complicated and messier as you move along, so you need to first tweak and then update the plan to keep it meaningful. Business plans must change as the world evolves and changes. As this happens, your plan needs to lead, not follow, that change. Built-in flexibility will allow you and your team to work with a plan that can meet these challenges. Let's look at the list of decisions facing you as you create a business plan that will have real meaning.

Determine First Things First; Decide Who Is Going to Write the Plan

An amazing number of otherwise sophisticated and stalwart business founders stammer and stutter or agonize and procrastinate rather than attempt to write their own plan. While you may fear that a homespun plan will not stack up well in comparison to those done by the pros, more often than not the opposite is true. The unmistakable slickness of professional plans or "stock" versions jumps out at sophisticated reviewers every time.

Looking to professionals to do the dirty work is not always the right answer. In choosing this route automatically, you do yourself a disservice. The most powerful of all business plans are those with the unmistakable imprint of the founders.

If you see the plan as a necessary evil required to get funded by the bank, outside investors, government bodies, or venture capitalists, you have missed the mark. If that were true, any good "boilerplate" plan on the shelf would do. You cannot merely substitute your data, personnel, and focus into a boilerplate and have it represent you well.

First, assemble the team (even if you determine the team is you alone) who will have the responsibility for writing the plan. The team members will dictate the perspectives that will define the version they create. So the writing team should be well considered to get the results you want.

Determine initially what the intent is for the version being created. Depending on who the creators are, your results will vary in thoroughness, timeliness, and emphasis on creativity, technology, or personality of the organization.

Determine Whether Your Plan Will Be Democratic or Autocratic in Design and Input

Begin by determining if this is to be a democratic or autocratic plan. If democratic in its design, just how democratic do you want it to be? Who *exactly* will write it? Diverse input may be admirable, but there will also come the time when decisions need to be made, to get it out of the conceptualization and engineering stage and move on to presentation.

Will it ever be finished? Are *you* "finished" yet? No. Your plan won't be either, because it represents a growing, changing set of criteria, players, environment, and focuses. As the various versions are ready for sharing, just accept that they represent the best picture at a frozen moment in time.

Build on and Customize Your Plan on the Basis of a Solid Foundation

A bare-bones version of similar businesses or other successfully founded and funded enterprises may be a good place to begin. Study what your predecessors and/or competitors have done. You might learn something—good and bad. Then customize your own plan by layering on *your* particular unique strengths and weaknesses as an organization, a management team, and leaders and innovators in your industry.

Create Different Versions for Your Internal and External Purposes

Varying versions of your business plan will exist for a variety of reasons. One or more critical versions will be prepared primarily to make critical presentations to potential financiers. That will require calling a halt to the engineering of the plan, pulling it off the drawing board, and declaring it "the plan" (at least for this particular need).

Another reason for multiple versions may be to accomplish varying tasks for which the plan may become a useful tool (i.e., marketing your business, educating potential second- or third-round financiers, acquiring a new supplier). Yet another is that a different version may put the emphasis on the syllable a particular party needs to hear about your business or team.

Vary the Emphasis on the Internal Versions

Your particular version might also look a bit different from the one in the hands of the vice president of marketing or head of research and development. Each of these key players has different perspectives and wears different colored glasses through which they read and interpret the plan. Just be sure that *you* are looking through very clear, very clean ones! You, as the responsible leader, are the final seal of approval on the finished product. Remember, too, that there never really will be a "finished" version, as variations in focus, management, design, business environment, research breakthroughs, and so on make for new and improved versions!

Have Professionals Review, Criticize, and Modify the Versions to Be Presented to Outside Parties

Allowing professionals to give your carefully constructed plan a professional look by reviewing, editing, and beefing up is fine. Such additional effort is desirable to achieve a finished product that will elicit positive responses from those sorely needed outside sources. Just remember, it is *your* plan. You want your views, your perspectives, and your values to come shining through the words, pictures, and other images.

Any version completed by an outside professional to give it that polished look will be current only as long as it takes the ink to dry. Remember, if it looks *too* slick, it won't be taken seriously. Investors are not dummies.

They will be looking carefully to see how well your own definition of the business; of the team; of your uniqueness; of your competition; of the size, depth, and lifeline of the business; and of your abilities to *make some serious money* in your stated business stacks up. First, the potential investors will look for it in the plan. If you get lucky, they will also give you the chance to do a live presentation.

If you do choose a professional to either pen or tweak the plan for you and your team, get ready to revise, update, and trash from the outset any unnecessary slickness or overly stylized descriptions. Merge the versions, if you must. But my advice is to come out in favor of input from your own key players who are closer to the action and may have clearer vision, if not linguistic skills.

Write Your Own Updated Versions

Keep in mind that the real "guts" of this plan are intended for heavy wear and tear. The operating version of the business plan is likely to become somewhat dog-eared and altered so dramatically in these fast-paced times that the business plan in year five may hardly resemble that in year one.

In creating these updated versions, you may most effectively utilize the input from a broader spectrum of participants. I suggest you get input from at least three members of your management team.

Using different combinations of personalities and organizational positions also adds strength to the finished product. One effective strategy allows all team members to take responsibility for one area they choose as their strongest suit and one of their weakest areas of expertise. This does a number of interesting and highly effective things for both the draft and the communication between critical team players.

First, each gets an opportunity to shine in his or her chosen area of expertise. The final product should, therefore, represent your endeavor in the best possible way. When two or more players deign an area as theirs, I suggest you let them collaborate. See what results!

You will learn just how expert your experts may be. You will know how well they interact with one another, how well they communicate with each other, how they individually gather supporting documentation or otherwise arrive at their conclusions, and how well their knowledge base and experience translates into an effective, highly desirable part of the overall plan.

Second, by having each team member spend time and energy on a second area in which they are not an expert but that is crucial to the successful functioning of the organization, you will get some fresh ideas and perspectives. These individuals normally will gain empathy, if not an outright understanding, for areas beyond their current focus.

This also lays the groundwork for cross-culturalization of expertise in your operation, a trait that is gaining in both popularity and necessity as organizations increasingly require all team members to wear multiple hats. As an insightful management and planning strategy, this will speak volumes to your investors of your team's foresight and cooperative strength.

With multiple people, personalities, and agendas involved in creating the updated business plans, you may well ask, how long is this process likely to take? The answer is as long as it takes.

Just as with your very first version of the plan, you must decide when updated versions have been engineered, reengineered, and reengineered again to the point of satisfaction to allow you to declare it *done*. With all these cooks in the kitchen, at some point (and only you will know when that point has been reached) you must declare it "soup!" and get on with it. Just remember, that for all the hassle, multiple input creates a stronger, better designed plan.

Make the Information Complete and Credible but Not Overwhelmingly Technical or Esoteric

Even if your strength in product and/or personnel is highly technical, don't get carried away! Including esoteric language and substantive technical material in the body of the plan may lead to controversy or, worse, undue emphasis on only technical rather than all substantive matters. Those plans that include detailed or complex technical data should position the intense, lengthy descriptions of such complex information in an appendix, with a relatively brief overview in the body of the plan.

Provide enough of the highly technical information to make the plan credible, but not so much that it will overwhelm the reader or detract from other important considerations. This allows the most detail-oriented, highly trained, and knowledgeable readers to have a field day in esoteric matters that are of keen interest to them. It also gives those less technologically inclined a sense of your uniqueness and *your* knowledge without becoming intimidated or put off about their own lack of knowledge.

Now you have some clear guidelines. You have made some critical decisions and are ready to begin. It is time to put ideas to paper, pen, audio, and/or video (depending on how high-tech your varying versions will be). Let's discuss what actually has to go into this plan. The components are:

What business you are in.

What makes you unique.

Who comprises the management team that will make it happen.

What will make the plan succeed.

What sales and profit margins you need to make it happen.

What the risks are for the investors.

WHAT BUSINESS YOU ARE IN

This may sound simplistic because *you* know what business you are in and it should be obvious to the world. Unfortunately, sometimes it is not even obvious to the founders. Too often, investors decry the tangle through which they must plow to uncover whether or not the enterprise is actually a business or just another new product.

If you are launching a series of new products or services, be they sequential or corresponding, be sure you and your team know what business you intend. It is not unusual to have a product introduction become the basis for a new division. This may or may not be in alignment with the overall mission, purpose, and plan. It may be just a side venture.

Another important element to this underpinning of the plan is to deliver focused facts versus generalizations or opinions in the description of the business, the existing and future market, the competition, and the anticipated forecasts for industry growth.

For example, a broad statement that you are in the computer software business does not clearly identify what you intend to do.

Specifying that your business is that of educational software for on-line purposes for the privately funded higher education market clarifies the business and the niche you intend to pursue.

Also, be aware that opinions hold little weight. Facts backed up with documentation and thorough research do! Make sure the essential information, in all six of the key elements of your plan, is included, is honest, and is organized in such a way that it is both readable and understandable to outside parties.

By the way, beginning with the discussion of your business and throughout the dissertation, I strongly suggest you avoid the use of industry or insider jargon. If you do avoid it, you will have sidestepped one of the six most frequently committed blunders in the writing of plans.

WHAT MAKES YOU UNIQUE

No one cares if the business you outline is growing at an exponential rate and offers unheard of returns on investment and professional growth opportunity if you don't bring something new to the table. Ask yourself if what you bring, be it product, service, delivery, people, and so on, will matter to the existing customer base and if it will be attractive to a growing and/or new customer base.

This is often one of the areas in which business plan writers have a serious tendency to overstate their case or exaggerate their particular advantages.

For example, if your particular advantage is reducing delivery time of your service by 50 percent from that of your competitors, it may be a significant advantage and make you unique (at least for a while). On the other hand, it may be inconsequential, even in the short run. If it is the only advantage you have, it may be far too weak a business advantage to wrap an entire business around. If your unique claim to fame is a 5-hour delivery time versus 10 (i.e., Federal Express's initial competitive advantage) in an industry that can fully utilize those additional 5 hours, you probably have something. If your unique delivery is 5 minutes versus 10 (i.e., in-store photo processing) and the 5-minute saving is virtually meaningless to the customer, it may not be worth the risk to pursue.

Your uniqueness needs to be stated clearly, candidly, and conservatively to be taken seriously. Only when your uniqueness is presented in this light will it carry any *credibility.*

Your unique advantage may be team (in-house and/or networks), proprietary process, cost, technological advantage, lead time to market, business connections, established manufacturing and/or distribution networks, leading-edge research, or "that no one else has entered the market yet." If it is the last on that list, be prepared. If it is the viable, lucrative market you believe it to be, you are not alone.

Knowing precisely who are your competitors is not the most important issue. What you should know is how much time, money, and expertise it will take to create serious competition for you and *when*. If it is not *who*, it may be *when*. If not *when*, it may be *where*. If not *where*, it may be the evolution or innovation *what*. Don't forget that. Competition always exists. It is your responsibility to know *who, when, where, what,* and *how* it will come.

Of the six major blunders both inexperienced and experienced entrepreneurs tend to repeat, two that tend to surface in discussing your unique qualities are: to be overzealous and/or to underestimate competitors, existing and potential

I would love to tell you that serious investors (venture capitalists, angels, and investment bankers) never chase deals or get caught in a feeding frenzy over unique new products or services. That wouldn't be entirely true. While the *vast* majority of the time you chase the money much more than it chases you, occasionally investors do go temporarily insane and fund "me-too" companies. This usually happens in what they perceive to be hot, nearly unstoppable markets. Most of the time this turns out to be a poor call because such markets rarely have staying power or depth.

Such insanity has hit more than once in the past two decades. Biotechnology, gene-splicing companies (good and bad) were funded despite miserable cash flow projections for years, and computer software has seen flameouts as well as success stories. If you are not unique but still have the burning desire to get outside funding, your best bet is to have impeccable timing to hit one of these periods of feeding frenzy.

For the other 98.7 percent of the time, you must rely on the tried and proven means to raising capital successfully—your unique advantages. Those elements that set you and your organization apart from the rest of the crowd should be *very* significant.

If your claim to fame is that you can improve productivity 10 to 20 percent over your closest competitor, you are in for some serious disappointment regarding funding. Investors are looking for something special.

Incremental differences, no matter the industry, will not do it. Innovation will! To be considered truly unique, you should target hurdling over the competition not in mere degrees but in entirely new dimensions. Looking into the future two years hence and creating it today is innovation; incremental pricing variations, delivery changes, or enhanced color or model selections is not.

You might be considered a serious candidate for funding if you could deliver a new product, competitive in your marketplace, in two weeks, for a cost of $25,000 when it takes your competitors a year and costs them $500,000!

Another highly rated method of establishing unique positioning for a company is the makeup of the management team. If you include in your ranks founders of proven, accomplished entities in the same or related fields, you have a good chance of standing out from the riffraff. That alone may be your ace in the hole and enough to warrant funding.

What makes ideas unique is, ultimately, their implementation.

Good management teams help set a foundation for credibility relative to the entire plan. Because there is so little room for error in the marketplace today, investors are truly seeking an unfair advantage on this front. They want the best you can get. And they want to know they can and do work together as a team.

WHO COMPRISES THE MANAGEMENT TEAM THAT WILL DRIVE THE PLAN TO SUCCESS

In addition to the founders, the crux of successful implementation of the plan will fall on the shoulders of the management team you have and/or will obtain. Who these people are and their proven ability to deliver are crucial to any good plan. Your candid descriptions, thoroughness, clarity, and emphasis of the strengths of sought-after candidates and/or positions is imperative.

Three of the six blunders to avoid in writing the plan are frequently committed in this section. One is to lie or cover up for perceived weaknesses. Another is the tendency for the founders to overstate their own value to the company. The third, a reality especially in the early stages of many young companies, is nepotism.

If current members are filling two or more slots while you search for the right players or the funding to bring on identified resources, indicate that. Over time the management team will expand as well. This is also the section to indicate what criteria you intend to use in seeking the best candidates for critical positions.

A few words to the wise about your management team, the description of it, and reasons to beef it up: *If you are weak in this area (management), you can kiss funding from venture capital groups and serious investment bankers and angels good-bye.*

Management is the item ranked most important by these funding sources. (Ranked second is the financial part of your plan on how to accomplish what you are setting out to do.) While great management teams alone would not seem to merit the unbalanced weight they are given (at least to the untrained eye), they do, and for good reason.

Prior experience is one thing. Successful entrepreneurial accomplishments are quite another. Best bets on nearly all venture capital lists are those founded by previously successful entrepreneurial start-ups, particularly when the players come in combination. Investors tend to believe companies led by successful entrepreneurs stand the best chance of getting past the ranks of the 80 percent failures and also-rans into the ranks of superstardom.

Those companies that will face the toughest, longest, and most rigorous uphill battle in securing funding for their launch or expansion are those with inexperienced founders and/or with management teams comprised of individuals who have had little or only modest success in the entrepreneurial arena. Serious money backers are not in the business of funding on-the-job training. They are placing their money on proven winners!

Those companies compiling management from both "old-line" corporations and "leading-edge" fast-paced growth companies stand the best chance of all, both for funding *and* for lasting, successful accomplishment. While the clash of corporate cultures within such organizations can be tantamount to World War III at times, when communication and respect are mutual and openly shared, the best of both worlds makes for the ultimate outcome.

WHAT WILL MAKE THE PLAN SUCCEED

You will note that this is fourth, *after* your team. Because the management team is so crucial to the success of your venture, members should be intimately involved in developing the plan on how to succeed. The strategies and timing of the steps to achieve your goals will be led by the management team you have on board as well as those you will add over the life of the enterprise. Their input, perspectives, and direction define the implementation of the idea.

In this section of your plan, you should discuss the particulars of the business that will make it operate successfully and what it will take to fund each component. This includes answers to all of the following:

- What are the key elements that must be addressed (all elements that are fundamental and cannot be overlooked in operating any sustainable business within your chosen industry)? This should be a brief but thorough discussion of the basics that make up the "skeleton" that you can then fill in with your particulars.
- How much will it cost? When? Why?
- What and how costly are the contingency plans?
- What are options or luxuries in the planning and strategizing process?
- What are the pitfalls to be avoided?
- What are the currently held beliefs regarding the importance of developments in this industry? (You can reference trade journals and industry experts.)
- How and when will you implement or find "secret weapons" to maximize benefit for the enterprise? (This is another form of contingency planning.)
- What will you do differently from the competition? Why? What makes you think it will (1) work, (2) make a difference, (3) be sustainable, and (4) provide you the lead or edge you want?

This is also where you should discuss that all-important ingredient to any operation's success—*the customer.* Who is *yours?*

Answer the following questions and you will thoroughly understand the size and potential of the market you are targeting. The result is a complete description understandable by all.

- What are they (existing and potential customers) looking for from you?
- Is there a difference between what they think they need and what they actually want?

- If so (and that is usually the case), how does your organization plan to address both?
- What makes you so sure your product, service, and business will satisfy them?
- Is the customer in flux as well? If this is a growing, or shrinking, customer base, how will it be defined one year, two years, five years out?
- Which sector will you be addressing? Are you moving with or against the customer profile?

These are just a few of the questions you might apply to your customer in-depth review. Yours should be customized as well, as thoroughly as possible, to discuss your own business. The heart of the plan to make the "plan" work focuses on what you have to offer and *who* and *how* your offering will satisfy.

Sometimes I find it amazing how businesses are started with the greatest of intentions and enthusiasm, without a thought as to *who* the customer is, might be, or whether or not they even exist. There are mighty few widgets in this world that are so magnetic that the world beats a path to the inventor's, founder's, or distributor's door. Without any plan to determine what customer will be best served by your business, how will you know who to bring your new invention, idea, process, or service to and get the response you want? This is a key element of the plan within the plan.

Once the customer is defined, what will be your process for redefining that customer over time, expanding the definition and parameters of sought-after customers, renewing customer loyalty, and maintaining an active customer base that exceeds industry standards in all criteria used to define "good" customers? That customer base may prove to be your greatest asset in years hence.

The serendipity of creating a customer base for your particular business is that with time, definition, and continued and growing customer loyalty, the customers themselves become an asset of the corporation. All you have to do is to complete your homework up front and then deliver the "goods" that make and keep the customers happy. Witness the chaos in today's marketplace in competition for the "communications-media" customer. Mergers and acquisitions abound in this and virtually every industry in which active, accurate, and well-maintained customer bases are cornerstones to new product or service introductions. Building the customer base, servicing it well, and enrolling the customer as a long-term "partner" in your enterprise creates the platform from which you may launch other products and services, even other businesses.

Customers are important because no matter how great our particular widget, someone has to *buy* it for us to get successful. We have to go out and actually *sell* these things (ideas included) if we hope to be successful in the capital sense. After all, investors may talk a good game about their empathy for your altruistic values and pursuits, but they never lose sight of the bottom line.

We are talking money here. Capital is invested because *more* capital is expected to come out at some point. The fact that this does not always happen (in fact, the majority of time it does *not* happen) makes investment sources demand even more from the would-be entrepreneur and his or her team. Their expectations are that only 1 in 10 enterprises they fund will be the superstars they seek. Yes, they are interested in your views on the customer. Even more important, they will go over your financial projections and pro formas looking for even the slightest inconsistency or erroneous assumption.

Just remember this. *To get money, it is imperative to show you will make money.*

WHAT YOU NEED TO DO TO MAKE
THE BUSINESS PROFITABLE

Profitability hinges on the sales your business needs and the profit margins inherent in those sales figures. Profitability is what leads to higher valuation of the company. Or at least that is the premise on which most organizations operate.

Investors are most concerned with the amount and timing of what *they* will make. They aren't against you and others (i.e., later-round investors) making money too, as long as they get theirs—first and foremost.

An important thing to remember is that they, more than you, will determine the best time for them to cash in their chips. The moment of truth will come when and if you actually come close to the pro formas you put forth now. Timing of the market entry with that of your corporate profitability is a tricky maneuver and not one you can entirely foresee at this stage.

Of course, everyone knows from the outset that pro formas are best guesses anyway. (You may ask yourself more than once in the years ahead, They *did* know that these were our best guesstimates, didn't they?) And those guesses are vitally important. For this, the fifth area, is the second most carefully scrutinized and analyzed section of your plan.

Financials, including projections (pro formas), constitute your presentation of what it will take to be profitable (aka successful). *Successful* then is defined as profitable, salable, and capable of offering shares to the marketplace through an initial public offering (IPO) or other means that allows for successful exit of the investor funds.

If you are already in business, you have existing historical data with which to begin, both for content and style. Remember to integrate the existing data with the forecasts in a meaningful and understandable fashion. If you are not in current operation, there are no *real* numbers, only those you and your team are about to throw up on the wall. How much of it will stick will depend on how conservative and realistic you are. Typically, entrepreneurs have a serious tendency to *overstate* their numbers rather than *understate* them. That is perfectly understandable. You are caught between a rock and a hard place on this issue. You want to get their attention in order to get the funding. If the numbers look ho-hum, they won't be interested. On the other hand, if the numbers look *too* good they won't believe them.

Investors want to be tantalized by the sizzle of your forecasts but they carry with them an inordinate amount of cynicism when it comes to supporting evidence for financial forecasts. So your mission is to forecast numbers with some believable level of optimism that can be logically supported.

The accuracy of forecasts for venture capital-backed companies is notorious. Yet this is the crucible for most business plans in the funding process. Knowing it is one of the most carefully considered parts of your plan, you should put every effort into making this section one that helps you stand out from the competition. Think of it this way: The financing group has a hundred plans before them to consider and all are in a business they understand well; and all have one or more significant qualities that make them unique. If *you* were in *their* shoes, which plan would get your attention? The one where the entrepreneurs paid short shrift to the financials or the one in which serious effort has been taken to provide well-considered, well-supported, well-presented financial data that is easy to read and understand?

Three separate segments of your financial reporting make up the pro formas. The most overlooked or misunderstood by entrepreneurs is the cash flow statement. Cash flow is *not* the same as income. The income statement, or profit and loss statement, is the second element. The third is the balance sheet. While the balance sheet is often only a formality for the fledgling start-up company, it is suspect if one is not included. For any company contemplating any serious debt financing, it is imperative. The caution here is again not to overstate the value of "goodwill" or other nebulous assets.

Financial forecasting is the one area where it can certainly pay in the long run to get professional help. A Big Six accounting firm's stamp of completion (if not approval) holds considerable weight with serious financiers. If you cannot afford such a full-blown relationship, bringing on a certified public accountant to help you prepare the documents is a very good idea. As your plan changes, it is highly likely the financials will also require alteration. Be prepared for several revisions should you face possible funding from a wide variety of potential suitors, alter the amount of investment capital you seek, or revise the structure of investment capital (which may or may not lead to more complex intermingling of structural alternatives).

Typically, five years of projections are provided. The first three, in my estimation, are the most important. In such a rapidly changing world, it is nearly impossible to accurately predict five years into the future. These projections reflect your way of thinking, your focus, and your perspective. Once you and the team in each department have forecast best case, worst case, and best guess numbers, discount them! Before you ever get in front of a potential investor with those numbers, use them for major target practice within your operation. Anything that cannot be substantiated or based on logical progression should be added to the best case scenario.

Even in the first year, there is a tendency to overstate the sales projections. More important the majority of founding fathers and mothers have blinders on when it comes to forecasting the cash flow, especially in this first year. The truisms are these:

Cash flow in high growth businesses is borderline positive/ negative.

Cash cows are mature, not growing businesses.

If you don't understand that, if you forecast great cash flow once you receive the investment backing you seek, you may not truly understand your business. Forecasting such a situation tells potential investors you have been, at best, sloppy in your thinking. At worst, it tells them you do not understand that fueling high growth requires continual major costs, research and development, and future financings.

Such costs have escalated more in recent decades due partially to the rate of change. To stay competitive in a world changing at the rate ours will in the coming decades, heavy investment in research and development will be required in virtually every type of business. To forecast anything less than 20 percent of your operating budget may be wishful thinking. In some industries, as much as 40 to 50 percent is not uncommon.

One more thing about the cash flow forecasts. Taxes are an important item. Inexperienced business founders often work with pretax numbers. This is a mistake. Taxes are here to stay and must be considered.

Once again this may require a specialist (a good tax accountant) to help assess the best possible strategies for your particular organization. Determining strategy beforehand, based on profitability and/or cash generation, does a great deal to build credibility *and* value. Maximizing use of the cash within the company is rarely done without forethought. Remember, too, that there are a variety of taxes to include in your numbers. A surprising number of budgets fail to include unemployment, inventory, sales taxes, and the like. And they do add up!

Relative to your profit and loss statement (P&L), a couple of important considerations are your forecasted cost of goods sold and the anticipated sales price. Realistically, not many products or services increase in terms of the price the market is willing to pay. Unfortunately, your additional costs borne in increased marketing and/or selling costs as well as increasing inflation are more likely to squeeze your profit margin over the life of each product and service you introduce.

Your margin of profitability is usually the best it will ever be the day of introduction of the product or service.

You may also want to provide an addendum to your P&L for the potential investors, one in which you remove any depreciation from your numbers. Many financiers are looking for the "real operating potential" that is based only on hard numbers. While depreciation is a "soft" line item that has "hard" results (i.e., tax savings), it is not an out-of-pocket expense. This is particularly important for businesses in which significant holdings such as real estate can have a significant impact on the operation of the entire enterprise. (Review *what business you are in.* This might be eye-opening for you as well.)

The last important ingredient of the dish you are cooking up is leveling with investors about the potential risks. This is your time to shine regarding the contingency plans you have devised, the foresight you have relative to potential problems on the horizon or even out of view.

WHAT RISKS EXIST FOR THE POTENTIAL INVESTOR

Don't make the possibility, even the probability, of risk come jumping off the pages at them. Just let them know how and why you evaluate their potential risk in *your* venture as you do.

This is where it pays in the long run to be candid. If there is something you have glossed over or someone on your management team whom you have falsely represented; if you have overstated your link to a major supplier; if there is a problem with a patent or other "ownership" issue of proprietary property; if you downplay the competition or denigrate their technology or management team or style, you will be "dead" as far as the funding sources are concerned.

Sophisticated investors understand risk. If they didn't, they would not be talking to you. They like to take what they consider to be "moderate" risk. The risk of a new venture, an untried product or service, an expansion into a new part of the world is offset by the strength that comes from your management team, understanding of the business opportunities, and the financial projections. Risk is heightened when you keep any important item in the dark.

The investment source is taking the risk based, first, on you and your management team; second, on the market opportunity and how well the investor determines you can seize it; and third, on your thorough and substantiated forecast of end results.

After going through the decision-making steps and then completing all six components of content outlined here, you now have a plan.

In the next chapter we will discuss the financial plan needed to fund and sustain the plan. While it becomes part and parcel of the business plan, the financials are important enough to warrant separate attention. While most entrepreneurs would rather avoid this topic, taking the mystery and pain out of their compilation is a challenge worthy of our discussion here.

CHAPTER 4

Financials That Actually Mean Something

I have read numerous business plans. You can
immediately tell which ones show original thought
and have been written by the founders and which
plans have been developed with off-the-shelf formats
or contracted out to a professional business plan writer
who had no clue as to the nature of the business that
was being planned. The projections in plans I've seen
are often unrealistic. These folks shouldn't be starting a
company; they should be writing science fiction or
romantic fantasy.

Alan Reedy

Tax attorney
(Newport Beach, California)

The importance of understanding and presenting financials, both projected and actual, in securing capital for your organization cannot be overstated. *Financials are ranked second only to the management team in the overall evaluation process by venture capitalists and sophisticated angel investors.* Thus, providing best "guesstimates" is a tricky and yet crucial component of the presentation you will provide to potential outside sources.

Creating numbers is an enlightening undertaking for you and the other founders and key management personnel. The underlying assumptions and the supporting documentation for the numbers in your financials are clear indications of your grasp of reality. Your fundamental business beliefs and your astute assessment of creative solutions to accomplish and maintain growth will be reflected in the numbers themselves as you are required to back them up through the assumptions you make.

Any numbers will do as long as they can be rationally supported and/or justified. If your corporate performance comes within 10, even 20 percent, of your forecast, you will be doing quite well. Most forecasts don't come close to the mark.

A forecast that is put together with at least some semblance of rational assumption is required by funding sources. And going through the process will benefit you and the other founders. The numbers you ultimately pen to paper become your initial road map or target for productivity.

OPTIMISTIC PROMISE

The presentation of your financial picture and forecast should leave an impression of optimistic promise for the enterprise, while simultaneously providing a realistic assessment of capability. To do this effectively you must consider variables that can and will affect your performance. In other words, you need to highlight the full potential of the organization through the numbers without overstating the possibilities. This is challenging for any business owner or entrepreneur.

Because of founders' built-in optimism concerning their business enterprise, it is easy for them to jump chasms of believability when it comes to market share, competition, price and profit points, and extended shelf life of whatever they offer. Such leaps of faith are not as easy for outside parties.

But well-planned and articulated financials can help investors make that leap. Without the rhetoric or hand waving that often accompanies in-person presentations on this particular subject, numbers on a page, disk, or computer screen must appeal to the logical minds of the readers.

Doing your homework thoroughly in creating financial forecasts does *you* the biggest favor of all. With financials based on well-researched cornerstones, you give your endeavor its best opportunity for true success. If you gloss over the numbers it will take to be truly successful or fail to uncover the likely potential hazards, you can shoot yourself in the foot from the very beginning.

Financial ruination can usually be determined early enough to take adequate measures to correct course. This is only true, however, when the planners are well versed on the basis for the original forecasts and understand the viable alternatives.

Without clear knowledge of financial conditions and possibilities as they truly exist, as opposed to those only in the wishful mind of the creator, management will operate in a self-imposed vacuum. This proves to be the case far too often. A commonly held misbelief is that capturing market share is the most critical element of creating financial success. Market share is only one element of the success formula.

CAUSE AND EFFECT

Owners and managers who do not understand the principles of cause and effect relative to financial decisions are highly susceptible to stagnant growth, lower profitability, and financial ruination. This simple fact of life is lost somewhere along the line in many organizations.

Understanding and dealing directly with the critical financial data and significant ratios is not a luxury in the marketplace today. *It is an absolute necessity.* The vast majority of entrepreneurs have little, if any, formal training in business economics. While such training is certainly no guarantee of business success, an understanding of some of the basics will save much time and many headaches in the decision-making process.

Accountants, credit managers, bankers, and business brokers, but rarely business owners and entrepreneurs, are well versed in cause-effect analysis represented through the eight basic ratios most widely used in accounting circles. The good news is that they are relatively straight-forward and any entrepreneur can learn them. Here they are:

1. *The quick ratio* is the fast, easy way to eyeball the company's current financial health. To calculate this ratio add the cash, short-term investments, and accounts receivable; divide by the current liabilities. At one time this was referred to as the "acid test" or "acid ratio." No longer. The oversimplification of depending on this ratio alone led many an analyst and business owner to ignore or overlook other important ratios (to be discussed in the following pages).

   This ratio differs from a comparison of total current assets to current liabilities in that it does not include inventory liquidation. As most business owners are well aware, inventory may not be immediately salable in either the time frame or at the price point one might wish. This becomes particularly true when the corporate back is to the wall and liquidation is required.

   Utilization of assets dramatically influences the true corporate financial profile. Whether or not such utilization is recognized and balanced in the operations of the company on a day-by-day, week-by-week, month-by-month basis influences the working capital and cash flow of the company. Thus, the quick ratio in conjunction with the other short-term asset utilization ratios makes up the "polaroid" shot of the company's financial feasibility.

2. *Net profit to net sales* is the ratio that quickly and effectively illustrates the company's ability to make a profit on the goods and services it provides. Other terms are sometimes used to describe this ratio—return on sales ratio, net profit margin, and the bottom line.

   Whether innocently or not, this number is sometimes misrepresented. Note the net in these numbers. Beware utilization of *gross to gross* numbers. There are far too many opportunities for leaks to make such a comparison of much value.

   Net profit to net sales is perhaps the best measurement of the company's ability to generate profit on its normal, day-to-day sales dollar. Most often this calculation is presented as a percentage rather than as a ratio. Thus, to calculate the ratio, divide the net profit by net sales, then multiply by 100 to achieve a percentage. For example:

Sunrise Company sold $6,000,000 in widgets this year.
Of the $6,000,000, $1,000,000 was returned as damaged goods.

$$\text{Gross profits} = \$2,000,000.$$
$$\text{Net profits} = \$550,000.$$
$$\text{Net profit to net sales ratio} = \$550,000 \div \$5,000,000$$
$$\times 100 = 11\%.$$

While the *true* bottom line is net profit after taxes, net before
taxes is the number most often used by bankers and investment
types. If you represent yours as an aftertax ratio, be sure to highlight this difference in your reports. Make it as simple as possible for any potential investor or other resource perusing your
report to pick up on the difference, especially if your number is
a particularly strong one for your industry.

3. *The collectible accounts receivable* ratio is the ratio that indicates the time required to collect cash from the sales generated.
This ratio is one of the most crucial for a business owner or
manager to understand and heed. This ratio provides an immediate analysis of the company's prospects for continued existence.
It is the indicator of the cash flow into the company to sustain
operations. This ratio is sometimes known as the "day's sales in
receivables."

The ratio itself simply indicates the average number of days it
takes to convert a sales receivable into cash. There are two critical aspects of a sale: the price and the collection of payment for
it. This ratio tells you when (and sometimes even *if*) you will get
paid for what you sell. The sales alone are good, necessary, and
highly desirable. Getting paid for the goods and services provided
is *imperative.*

To get the number, multiply the accounts receivable number
by 365, then divide the result by net sales.

Remember, you are seeking low ratios. Low ratios indicate
solvent, responsible customers; less expense in recordkeeping
and collection personnel; and reduction in the probability of
loss as slow-moving accounts turn into bad debts. Historically,
the common range has been one to two months. This can be
misleading regarding small organizations, however. Small businesses selling into larger organizations often find their range

more like three to five months. In your own endeavors, check this ratio at regular intervals and track whether there is a particular type of customer whose delinquency causes your ratio to get out of gear. This ratio is an important early warning signal of possible financial trouble.

4. *Net sales to total assets* is the ratio that allows you to effectively assess utilization of all your corporate assets in generating profits. Sometimes other terms are used to describe this ratio, such as *asset utilization ratio* or *asset management ratio.*

To calculate this ratio, divide the net sales figure by total assets. As with the net profit to net sales ratio, the higher the number, the lower the financial leverage.

When total assets are utilized ineffectively or without immediate financial return applicable to their existence, the leveraging the owners face can be substantial. The majority of businesses in the past have found this ratio to be in the 2.0 to 3.0 range. But as we approach the turn of the century, higher ratios are more prevalent and indicative of better utilization of hard capital resources. As more and more "virtual" companies emerge, the balance sheets will reflect less and less real estate and long-lived capital equipment among their major resources.

Assets are taking on new character today as the emphasis in our world shifts from physical assets to mental assets. Rules that have applied in the past to corporations that operate with a manufacturing mentality are not as effective or meaningful for companies emphasizing intellectual properties. As such a shift in consciousness occurs, timeworn means of evaluating financial strength will be tested and converted to reflect such change.

Using the earlier example, this ratio for our fictitious company would look like this:

Sunrise Company's current assets = $1,000,000.
              Long-term assets = $6,000,000.
Net sales of $5,000,000 ÷ total assets of $7,000,000
                              = ratio of nearly .71.

This means Sunrise's managers should quickly assess the underemployment of the company's resources. Creating a plan to better utilize and deploy the assets at their command is essential to better leverage which ultimately directly affects the bottom line.

5. *Cost of sales to inventory* ratio is the indicator of merchandise turnover. Generally, the older the inventory, the less value, and the greater strain on the operation's cash flow.

This ratio expresses how many times inventory turns within the year. It is the measure of the company's control of inventory in relation to net sales. Historical numbers or comparisons of the ratios may not be as important to the business owner or manager as the trends for the particular ratios. It is another quick measure of the criteria that most affect the business.

To get the number, divide the cost of sales by the inventory.

For companies that do not maintain inventory, obviously this ratio is nonapplicable. But a certain elementary understanding of the principles is applicable. If you consider ideas, concepts, and service programs in the same light, similar conclusions can be drawn for the noninventory business enterprise.

Let's look at a couple of examples:

Company X is a retail food operation, doing $8,588,000 in sales. Their cost of sales is $5,786,000. Their inventory at year-end is $1,160,000. In this case, dividing $5,786,000 by $1,160,000 results in a ratio of 4.98.

Company Y, in the same industry, has sales of $7,644,000, cost of goods sold is $4,830,000, and the book value of their inventory at year-end is $1,090,000. In this case, dividing $4,830,000 by $1,090,000 results in a ratio of 4.43.

In these examples, while the sales, inventories held, and cost of goods are relatively close in value, Company X is doing a better job of moving its inventory through the cash cycle. If Company X were to further improve their competitive advantage they would be well-advised to reduce their inventory. Such a reduction, even by as little improvement as 15 percent, would bring their ratio up nearly an entire point to 5.86 (inventory would drop to $986,000). Such inventory would reduce possible loss due to damage, obsolescence, or potentially unsalable inventory (in other words, improve the financial position of the company and increase its return on equity).

High ratios are usually more favorable. Storage costs are lower because there is less to store with greater merchandise distribution. The costs and time of recordkeeping are reduced. Interest and carrying costs are lower as the sales reflect greater generation of cash. Obsolescence, loss, and deterioration are all characteristics of slow-moving inventories. By paying close attention to this ratio, you have an opportunity to avoid these pitfalls.

To achieve positive ratios of inventory turnover, the capital base and cash flow of the organization usually need to be solid. Those organizations operating with minimal cash flow or low capitalization may not have the same viability and opportunity to maintain and improve their inventory control and distribution. This is a good ratio to test that particular situation. Ordering costs are normally higher for companies whose ratios are high. Often they also encounter customer dissatisfaction with short-falls if they are not maintaining substantial inventories of popu-lar or advertised items.

Inventory turnover varies among industries but is usually con-sidered acceptable if it falls in the range of four or more times a year. However, four times can be far too few, especially when introduction of new products, new competition, new pricing, or new trends is fast-paced. In such cases, turnover of 6 to 10 times a year may be a better guideline by which to gauge your performance.

6. *Net sales to fixed assets* indicates the company's ability to gener-ate sales only from the use of its fixed assets. By calculating this ratio as well as the net sales to total assets discussed earlier, effective utilization of the current assets can also be extrapolated. When combined, the results of these ratios give the management team an effective basis for financial decision making for both day-to-day operations and annual budgeting.

This financial ratio is also known as the fixed assets activity ratio. Leveraging fixed assets to create current return is one method of lateral expansion useful in increasing business value. To get the number, divide net sales by fixed assets.

While high ratios indicate companies in which depreciation and interest costs are reduced, such organizations also tend to experience increased costs for operating leases, personnel, and delivery expenses. Weighing the choices available for your business by applying the results of these particular ratios is a far more enlightened process. Deciding to invest capital in fixed assets is much trickier today than ever before. Understanding these ratios allows for more effective use of assets and better decisions regarding the addition and/or utilization of personnel and space and location requirements for storage and operation of the business.

7. *Net sales to net worth* ratio is often referred to as the trading ratio. Sometimes this is also known as the investment adequacy ratio. It is calculated by dividing net sales by net worth.

This ratio measures the company's financial capacity to support its net sales volume. Without a substantial net worth to carry the company, the future of creating sales is a considerable risk. This fact is often overlooked by fledgling entrepreneurs, who sometimes succeed with low net worth. But getting away with such leveraging is unlikely to last over an extended period.

Low ratios reduce financial leverage while also reducing return on equity. Low ratios indicate high net worth relative to sales generated. In general, the more mature the company and/or the industry, the more you should expect lower ratios. Early years of the company are generally the most highly leveraged and create the highest return on equity. (To verify your confidence in your own position in relation to return on equity, check this result against the others that allow you to measure return on equity.)

There is no common range for this ratio. To get a good comparison, search the information available on your competitors and calculate their ratios. A ratio of 5 is not uncommon for many industry groups. On the other hand, a ratio of 80 or more is also a reality in some industries. Again, maturity of the company is a component in creating the lower ratio, as net worth accumulates and builds.

8. *Long-term liabilities to total noncurrent assets* is otherwise known as the long-term financing ratio. To calculate this ratio, divide long-term liabilities (those longer than one year to maturity) by total noncurrent assets (those which cannot be transformed instantaneously into either cash or other liquid form).

It is important to note the precise use of borrowed funds to calculate this ratio. Funds borrowed to finance acquisition of fixed and other noncurrent assets must be separated from long-term liabilities incurred for other applications to the capital needs of the company.

As we move toward the new century, fewer new organizations will find this ratio significant. As real estate takes on a lesser role, this calculation has less meaning. In fact, many mature companies are divesting such real estate and nonproducing non-current assets. Such divestiture allows them to take advantage of the appreciation that occurred in the past but today is slowing. Shedding noncurrent assets in the corporate portfolio also makes such entities less attractive as takeover targets for corporate raiders.

In many of the emerging growth businesses today, both the long-term debt incurred and the noncurrent assets of corporate balance sheets are taking on a new look. Assets and the funds to acquire them are increasingly of a shorter-term nature. For many existing companies in the throes of expansion and change, the newly acquired assets often tend to fall into this shorter-term description, as well.

While real estate served as a substantial benefit to the balance sheet of corporations over the past 50 years, today the financial return on dollars thus invested is far more questionable. While 8 to 20 percent annual appreciation was the norm throughout the past two decades, today forecasts are for a mere 2 to 3 percent appreciation on real estate holdings. With this in mind, more companies are deciding against long-term debt at a cost of 8 to 10 percent or more to invest in this type of asset.

Conservative, traditional investors and business pioneers usually consider high debt to be unfavorable. A high ratio, on the other hand, strengthens the company's working capital. In assessing this ratio for your company, high debt on nonperforming or declining asset values should be a wake-up call. Few organizations today can afford such luxury. Leverage is beneficial only when values improve. That is a key fact to keep in mind.

For the reasons outlined above, your particular corporate philosophy relative to the most productive means by which to build value in your organization will be reflected in this particular ratio. A ratio in excess of 1.0 indicates long-term borrowings in excess of book value of fixed assets and other noncurrent assets.

WHAT YOU SHOULD LEARN FROM
THE BIG EIGHT RATIOS

Your concern should be with the underlying meaning of the numbers, not in the *how* of the ratios. Apply these financial tests to decisions about the future to give yourself invaluable insight and keen competitive skills.

You can be more effective in your role as the founding entrepreneur, decision-point management member, lead sales generator, or other critical position, if you learn and understand these basics.

There is no reason to learn and understand how entries are put into the books and flow through the various accounting pages to accumulate summaries. You do not need to become an accountant. You do need to assume your rightful responsibility for maintaining fiscally sound assumptions on which the numbers are based.

Doing that effectively means understanding the reasons the numbers get generated in the first place and then measuring your forecasts and/or performance against some set of standards.

Trade associations have taken the lead in providing industry guidelines with which to compare your own numbers. But remember that such guidelines are simply that, a yardstick by which to measure your performance from time to time. In many companies and in many industries, new yardsticks are emerging, often with entirely different markings.

The results of taking the time and energy to understand the *what, when,* and *why* that back up the financials of your organization will be:

- Making decisions that have definable results appropriately anticipated rather than having results that are either inconsistent or surprises.

- Understanding how you stack up in comparison with others in your industry, allowing you to achieve higher profit margins than your competitors.

- Accurately assessing the essential trends and drawing meaningful conclusions in comparing your numbers with some set of industry standards.

- Communicating better with potential funding sources and with the financial professionals with whom you will deal in the day-to-day operation of your business.

Understanding these eight basic ratios of financial analysis will help management focus on the good, the bad, and the ugly of operational success long before "damage control" becomes an issue.

Remember this important point: *The ratios derived from the company financial statements will be meaningful only when applied in comparison to your own past performance in addition to the comparison to industry standards or norms.*

In that way, you, as well as investors and outside financial analysts, will be able to determine deviations that make you stand apart from the competition. It is important, therefore, to do your homework on an ongoing basis to determine just where the industry is and how key players, good and bad, are faring.

BENEFITS OF SOUND FINANCIAL FORECASTING

By understanding the implications of decisions as they relate to the financial bottom line, you will create forecasts and projections, as well as make better informed daily decisions, that will allow your organization to stay ahead in today's highly competitive world.

Other benefits accrue to you and your managers from learning, understanding, and being able to talk the language of financial ratios. These include:

1. More complete understanding will lead to more timely and usually better decisions in all areas of you business.
2. The better prepared you are, the more effectively time and money will be spent with the financial professionals.
3. The more effective use of these resources will relate to more effective financial decision making.
4. Those potential investors you seek will be tremendously impressed, and rightly so. (Gaining this financial skill will put you in the top 10 percent of all companies sophisticated investors meet!)

5. Your attention will be riveted to the key financial elements in business competition. Alternatives in each critical business decision can be weighed with meaning because they are more clearly defined and substantiated.

Often any substantive measurement is lacking when key decisions are made. Cause and effect return time and time again when you clearly understand the direct linkage and impact of decisions that might otherwise appear disjointed or only remotely related.

6. You gain the ability to test the validity of assumptions in internal reports and projections (budgets, cash flows, etc.). While one version of entrepreneurial style may be to test for validity merely by getting a majority to agree, the more scientific test can be applied. Even if the results of the test are incongruent with the final decisions, measuring and discussing the essence of validity strengthens the awareness of the key participants to the impact of the decisions made.

FINANCIAL CONSIDERATIONS DIFFER FOR LARGE VERSUS SMALL ORGANIZATIONS

Large, complex businesses virtually always have a full line of specialists. Such specialization means cross-training of division managers to acquire financial management skills rarely occurs. Even the largest and most prestigious organizations have rarely made such a bold move. To do so would create extraordinary new skills in multiple managers and levels—a concept considered revolutionary until now.

But, with the chaos caused in downsizing, the rate of change, and growing competition from around the globe as well as from small, guerrilla companies spinning off from the corporate giants, the strategy can no longer be ignored. Over 30 percent of the Fortune 500 of five years ago have fallen from those ranks. Thus, turnover in large corporations through downsizing, layoffs, and retirement programs creates a near-vacuum in trained personnel with financial management skills.

To successfully undertake such financial cross-training is still considered risky business. Risky or not, if you expect your business to survive and thrive in the coming century, that risk *must* be taken.

As decisions are made more readily, in a wider band of geographic locations, and at differing levels of management, such skills must be added to the arrows in the successful business manager's quiver. This critical skill of financial management will become increasingly demanded by the managers themselves while being recognized as critical to the organization's success.

In a small business, such financial management skill is not only advisable, it is also imperative to the staying power of the organization.

The majority of small businesses in the United States are staffed with three to five officers. These corporate officers are expected to wear many hats, but only in the rarest of organizations do *all* have at least a basic understanding of the impact of the basic financial ratios as they apply to their business.

The reasons for such thin ranks among financial specialists within the business organizations tend to fall into one of the following categories:

- The majority of founders and officers of small business come from the ranks of sales or production.
- There is not enough time to train all, or even a majority, of the management team because within two years of initial operation one in four new businesses either sells or ceases operations.

KEEPING THE BUSINESS IN BALANCE

In many organizations, the financial person's role is merely to keep the *books* in balance. The better approach is that of keeping the *business* in balance. To do this means understanding the meaning behind each listed asset and liability on the balance sheet and the significance of the income and cash flow statements. Then you can clearly prepare and understand the four resulting financial reports used in all businesses— the unaudited year-end statement, the quarterly report, the projected financial report, and the audited financial statement.

First, let's look at the balance sheet and the asset side of the ledger.

The Balance Sheet

Of all the types of assets, current assets are truly the important ones. This includes the following:

Cash

Cash is certainly easy enough to understand. The interesting but often undervalued or misunderstood correlation is that cash is directly related to cash flow.

Income statements and cash flow statements are not one and the same. Novice and experienced business owners alike know this but sometimes forget. Of *all* the many important financial elements to assess and watch with a careful eye, none is more important than the lifeblood of the organization, the cash that is flowing in and out on a daily basis.

The only caution is that by paying too much attention to this one element alone, it is easy to lose sight of the overall plan or strategy. So pay attention but know the difference between cash flow and income. Just make sure that enough is *actually flowing* while you are in pursuit of the bigger and better dreams for the company.

Accounts Receivable

Theoretically, accounts receivable will be turned into cash in a short time (one year maximum). Ten percent of sales is a relative good number to use in determining bad credit risk. Cash flow for a particular industry or company may require shorter fuses on the turn time on these receivables.

Inventory

Some percentage of all corporate purchases will remain in this category forever. Thus, real operating numbers may hold significantly less value than what you may actually carry on the balance sheet. *(Note: Being alert to this as a potential problem is one of the primary reasons for ratio analysis.)*

Liabilities

On the other side of the ledger are the obligations of the organization, the liabilities. Differentiating current liabilities from long-term ones is simply a matter of time. Current liabilities include all obligations due within the next 12 months. Again, this is pretty simple to determine.

Current versus long term is the most important focus for our purposes here. The caution I share is to not overlook any of the following as a current rather than as a long-term liability. All, for purposes of accurate financial reporting, are considered *current*.

- Any obligation that does not have a distinct maturity date.
- Tax liabilities or reserves.
- Advance payments or deposits.
- Declared but unpaid dividends.
- Contingency reserves.

The important integration of these current assets and current liabilities is the term *working capital.* Working capital is simply current assets less current liabilities. An adequate cushion between current assets and current liabilities is essential. Without it, management flexibility is nonexistent. *Again, something that seems so simple to understand is sometimes so difficult to implement.*

Little further need be said about income statements and cash flow statements other than to again remind you that they are two different animals. The first reflects the revenue versus expense, resulting in either a profit or a loss. The second reflects the lifeblood of the organization, for it is the statement of cash flowing in and cash flowing out. Without it (the *flow*), the business will come to a screeching halt. Now to those four reports.

The Unaudited Year-End Statement

This report is often prepared by accountants or bookkeepers or by the owner/entrepreneur in many small businesses. When *actual* operations and financial conditions are not accurately represented, problems begin to occur. Sloppy or inaccurate bookkeeping ultimately becomes a stumbling block for realistic understanding and appraisal of the company's operations and evaluation.

The timeliness of preparation is often overlooked by small businesses. This will not be the case once outside investors are involved. Serious investors expect quarterly reports within 45 days of the end of the quarter.

Investors tend to expect the annual unaudited report within 60 days of the end of the year. With accountants busy in that first quarter each year, the time and resources required to complete this report on such a timely basis can prove irritating and frustrating for everyone involved.

A word of advice is to determine up front how you will get the job accomplished, meaningfully, and to the satisfaction of your investors. Such knowledge is also highly critical to your ongoing operation and should not be allowed to languish while you and the other managers scramble to put out fires.

The Interim, Usually Quarterly, Report

The good news in privately held companies is that this report is not quite so critically reviewed as are those of publicly traded companies.

The importance placed on quarterly reports for publicly held companies can prove detrimental to the overall functioning of the business when results are less than anticipated or new developments make radical changes. Because perception becomes reality, the anticipation of the actual report often has more impact than the report itself.

Privately held companies are far less formal in this presentation. Investors will require complete disclosure of what is happening but tend to be less critical than when the day-to-day evaluation of their holdings is at stake.

Quarterly reports keep management and owners tuned-in to the reality of the business operations on a timely basis. This prevents operating in the dark about the bottom line while the business operators go on their merry way selling, promoting, building, servicing, and generally running the business.

These reports are checkpoints along the highway taking you from point A to point B. Without them, it can be easy to get off the right road and find yourself in unfriendly terrain, with little gas or other provisions to get you on your way.

The bad news is that quarterly reports come around very fast, require good records, and take time to produce. The good news is that they can become an effective operating as well as marketing tool.

My suggestion is to come up with a format that is simple, straightforward, clean, concise, and complete.

If you are bold enough, ask for investor feedback in any area covered. You will be amazed at the results. You are not obligated to listen, but in so doing, you may receive early input that can prove valuable or you may head off problems and upsets at a manageable stage.

The Forecasted or Projected Financial Report

This financial report is part of every iteration of the business plan, and it is the one most scoffed at *or* most referred to, depending on the reader's perspective.

Putting the forecast together can be torture or it can be great fun. Once completed, it is often the pride and joy of entrepreneurs, division managers, and project leaders. The numbers begin with "passable," move on to "probable," and end up at "possible."

Presenters zero in on the "possible" and tend to make that the *worst case* in their minds. The debt and/or equity partners, on the other hand, zero in on the "passable" and tend to make that the *best case* in their minds. Obviously, the solution is some happy medium ground. This is referred to as the "best guess" or "most probable" case.

The problem for those seeking the capital is that if they don't show the high-end, wildly optimistic view, creditors and investors will very rarely come to the same conclusions as the founders or generators of the plan. Further, once you provide such numbers in black and white, they tend to hold your feet to the fire later if you don't match them.

No one in his right mind relies on these forecasted numbers. They are only figments of someone's imagination, backed up in the best of cases with thoroughly documented support to warrant their existence. Whether optimistic or pessimistic, the numbers are drawn out of someone's hat and then the management team scrambles to justify the why, when, where, what, and how to give substance to the numbers.

Everyone within the organization wants to somehow believe that the only limitation to growth and prosperity is the sky or something closely approximating it. Most of the time no one really believes this, but some small part wants to leave the door open for the possibility.

Thus, if you are not showing best case, worst case, and most likely to potential investors (as well as to the management team), you may be doing yourself a disservice. Going immediately to realistic, as opposed to either end of the optimistic/pessimistic spectrum, takes much of the fun and the eager anticipation out of the process. Sizzle here, as in most things, is important if you hope to get people riled up and give them hope for unbounded success.

Both ends of the spectrum should be dealt with head on and evaluated. It is important for everyone involved in this process to understand the underlying critical reasons that make those numbers come together. And . . . surprise! . . . neither best case nor worst case numbers come about purely because of sales.

Projecting five years into the future is a fairly standard practice. As you ponder your own five-year forecast, consider the following:

- The amount of information that exists in the world today will more than double in that same time period.
- Technology will introduce new methodologies, products, and opportunities that do not even exist today.

- The marketplace for your goods and services will have shifted in ways unforeseen at the moment.

Projecting into the future for five years, three years, or even one is trickier now than it has ever been. Staying in sync with future trends, technological breakthroughs, rapid obsolescence of products, delivery systems, marketing avenues, name-brand recognition and acceptance, and a myriad of other fine details will mean the difference between the life or death of your project, division, or corporation.

Financial forecasting needs to be tightened up, tuned up, and revved up no less than every six months for it to become an effective tool in both your management plan and your capital plan. As this forecast changes (and it will), keep all critical players informed. Program in obsolescence and R&D results on a two- to two-and-a-half-year cycle.

The Audited Financial Statement

Audited financials entail a number of interesting elements. It is good practice to be aware of what the official accountant's opinion is likely to be.

What an audited financial represents:

1. This is a reliable review of the company's operating numbers for a specific time period (usually one year).

2. The certified public accountant (CPA) conducting the audit may express an unqualified opinion that the statement fairly represents the financial position and results of the accounting period in review.

3. The CPA may limit the scope of the opinion if there is incomplete information or she is unable to confirm all accounts.

4. The CPA may give an adverse opinion if the company did not adhere to generally accepted accounting practices.

5. The CPA may also give no opinion if he determines certain factors preclude presentation of an opinion.

What an audited financial statement is not:

1. This financial statement is not one of value or appraisal.

2. It is not a qualitative measure of the numbers or ratios considered appropriate to the business being conducted.

Audited statements are costly, lengthy, and likely to be required by sophisticated investors for privately held companies. They are required for all publicly traded corporations and entities. The most common range of time to conduct an audit in small corporations (under $5 million sales) is two to four months at a cost of $30,000 to $75,000.

It is imperative to the cash flow survival of your privately held company that you have budgeted correctly for this. Your true cost for the audit will include both the out-of-pocket expense and time and additional internal expense of employees to aid in the preparation and information gathering required. For most small businesses, this is one of the major endeavors of the entire year. It is not to be taken lightly and, more often than not, it is a humbling process for any business owner.

Financials . . . ah, yes. Do them with meaning and they will mean something. Do them casually, blindly, or incompletely and they will not be worth the paper they're written on or the time invested to create them!

CHAPTER 5

Structuring That Works for You and Your Money Partners

By altering the structure of our offering to bring the form of investment in alignment with the use of the funds, we were able to save equity and place the offering more quickly. That's money in our pocket by having stock left to sell at a higher price further down the road. Financial structuring is a critical piece for business executives to master.

Elorian C. Landers

Chief executive officer
Fyrglas, Inc.
(Houston, Texas)

How the company is structured may seem a simple matter. It can be. More often than not, however, simple solutions are temporary at best. The truth is that structuring the evolution of the company is an important factor to the success of the endeavor. Well-planned structuring enhances the capital raising, the team building, and the growth of the organization.

In this chapter we will review structuring to maximize benefits for you and your investors. The first part of that process is to consider the types of investment structure (the financing). Second, you need to carefully assess the timing of your capital needs. And, third, you must review and select the type or types of legal structuring that will work best for you.

What exactly is the *structure* of the organization? The structure is the integration of the method of financing and the legal organizational form of your business; for example, a debt offering for a C corporation.

The forms you choose must adhere to legal guidelines. Your selection of form will also impact both your operational decision making and the expansion of the organization.

The type of funding you select may influence the structure you ultimately choose. How funds will be utilized will largely determine the type of funding most appropriate for each funding level. The timing of the funding sought will also sometimes sway the structural choice.

For example, you might automatically choose to form the organization into a C corporation versus a limited liability corporation (LLC) (the legal structure). This decision should hinge on your choice of financing and timing, but in many circumstances these are overlooked in favor of selecting the legal format first.

Either way, you will have made choices, sometimes without even being aware of their implications. But those choices impact your operation on multiple levels.

In this case, your choice of C or LLC will impact how your investment opportunity is offered and will have differing tax ramifications for owners and operators. Liability of key participants, too, is an issue.

Both forms of organizational structure have their proponents and their detractors. Both also have some preconceived perceptions by various entities, including your vendors, customers, existing and future employees and managers, and potential investors.

One of the first lessons on structuring, then, is to understand that you and your key team have one set of determinants about your structure.

Your investors may have another. Your task is to find the one or more that work best for all key players.

RESTRUCTURING CAN BE COSTLY

In today's world, the structure of the enterprise often begins one way and ends another. This can be costly—both in terms of additional money and in time spent getting it right. Nonetheless, moving from one form of structure to another is done quite frequently and for a myriad of reasons. Another frequently used tactic is that of adding other structures as the progress of the organization demands. The implications of such restructurings can and will be as complicated as the reasons and the parties involved in their creation.

Far too often little, if any, attention is paid to how best to structure or organize the endeavor in the earliest stages. This is an important point lost on many entrepreneurs eager to just get started. The best procedure is to think far enough into the future to determine the most probable course and timing of growth.

In this way the organization can best be structured to maximize the potential for its own benefit. It will also allow solicitation of investment capital in the most intriguing and acceptable fashion. While the choices of structure are limited, the effect of selection can and will play an important role in the progress of the company.

For enterprises with multiple products, services, and even divisions, utilizing more than one form of structure, or at least preparing for them from the beginning, is often the answer. For companies on a fast track to success, well-conceived structuring can also become a magnet for multiple forms of investment capital.

With structural alternatives, simultaneous efforts for capitalization are often more readily accomplished as well. Today's environment in capital formulation affords better opportunity to customize your structure than ever before. Understanding the pros and cons of one over another, or using multiple structures as a strategy, is the hallmark of the entrepreneur of the new millennium.

How and why companies are created in the images they are is a function of the current thinking of the principals. If that thinking is based on lack of information and understanding of the importance of structural creativity, it can be equated to building a superstructure without substructure or forms.

STRUCTURING CHOICES AND CONSIDERATIONS

A hypothetical situation that illustrates various components of the process many young entrepreneurial companies go through follows below. Through this hypothetical situation we will investigate the various forms of structure and at least some of the ramifications of their inclusion in an overall capital plan.

Say you find yourself holding patent rights to a series of products that have merit on their own but could potentially be stronger if you were to join forces with other people who hold related patents. Before now, each organization, and the people within them, had worked independently. Now you think it may be time to centralize your efforts and your operations.

At this juncture you may form a new company around your cumulative patented products. By joining forces, you stand a better chance of competing in the world markets. You jointly expect to be able to bring more outstanding products to market in a shorter time period than many of the more staid, gigantic corporate competitors.

This will require you to launch and sustain an integrated organization capable of creating, developing, manufacturing, marketing, and managing the product under your joint domain. As you are, in effect, giving "birth" to a new entity, be aware that you are likely to need outsiders to manage and administrate this new entity.

Cumulatively, you and your new partner organization have invested months and years in the research, the prototyping, the testing, the patent and copyright work. You have done test marketing beyond your immediate group of friends to determine that there is a high level of interest in what has been created.

The question now is what form this new organization should take. Whatever the form (structure), it definitely will take money to accomplish your goals.

In most circumstances, entrepreneurs employ their creative energies to their highest and best use to create phenomenal new products while depleting whatever capital they have. The first avenue they follow once they have depleted their own resources is usually family and friends. It is when that money is gone that *real* outsiders will be sought.

The normal situation is one in which the inventor/entrepreneurs actually want to get their breakthrough products to market. They also want to get paid. Both objectives are real and understandable.

Often, from a structural perspective, the problem is that you now want to do it in the shortest possible amount of time. That becomes a problem because, without forethought, the route or structure selected may not be the best choice. In fact, it may not even be *one* of the best choices.

Often at this point you feel a sense of payback is long overdue. Entrepreneurs who know their creations will have a major impact on some significant portion of humankind usually want to be paid handsomely. How to structure the funds they need and want is often the least of their worries.

So you are thinking, "Whether we bring money into the fold to make this creation a reality by forming a C corporation, a LLC, a partnership, either general or limited, or establish a business trust, who cares? Let's just get it in here. *Now!*"

LEARN YOUR FINANCIAL STRUCTURING OPTIONS

Let me share some advice. Hold on to your optimism and your enthusiasm, but take a breather long enough to learn what you need to about structuring. It will pay handsome dividends. Another little secret is that if you don't think about the implications and importance of creative structuring, your investing partners will!

To determine what structure will work best, you need to understand what you will be expected to accomplish, what "type" of investment offering may make the most sense for your particular needs, and precisely how and when you will utilize any funds raised.

Following are the major activities that need to be accomplished in our hypothetical example of joining forces with another organization to create a new entity:

- Create a manufacturing division (or reach agreement with an existing one).
- Create a sales and distribution arm for the products created (or reach agreement with an existing one).
- Find or create customers (or reach agreement with someone who already has the "right" type of customer).
- Determine the price point and delivery time frame for the targeted client base (or reach agreement with someone who already has the market studies and R&D done).

- Develop repeat, sustainable customers who refer others
  because of product, service, and consistent performance.
  (This one is difficult to farm out! It is going to be up to you!)

Assume for the moment that the first levels of investment risk are relatively abated because you and your new partner organization each have funded your own R&D, investigated the viability and feasibility of your products (seed capital), and sustained yourselves in the process to date (working capital).

Doing what needs to be accomplished to launch and sustain an organization as outlined above is going to take substantial time and money. It also is unlikely that this will be a onetime shot. Generally, most successful corporate launches involve between three and five levels of funding.

In all cases the decision of structure will be made by people with a variety of perspectives and different value systems and agendas. First understand which alternatives most appeal to you and why. Then consider those choices most appealing to the other key players. This will allow you to choose with forethought the system or structure that will work best for your unique operation.

GUIDELINES FOR TYPE OF FINANCING

The first level of decision making facing you is the type of financing. Financing can be either debt or equity. It can be debt combined with equity. It can be debt converting to equity. It can be debt and equity offered simultaneously.

The type of financing is applied to all forms of corporate or partnership structuring selected. Often before the founders or management team select the style of structure they want, they need to determine what type of financing they feel comfortable accepting. In making this decision, don't forget to listen to your experienced advisors from the legal, accounting, and strategic viewpoints. Whichever combination you determine to use is what works for you!

Advantages of Debt Financing

There are certain advantages to debt that warrant your attention. The primary ones are these:

- Documentation costs are normally less for debt offerings.

- Equity ownership (of major importance to most entrepreneurs) is not diluted.

- The time required to actually secure debt financing often is considerably less than when seeking equity participation.

- The term and cost of the investment can be clearly established.

- The terms of the financing can be more clearly aligned to the appropriate needs of the organization.

- Measurable returns on capital invested can be clearly monitored.

Disadvantages of Debt Financing

There are some serious disadvantages to choosing debt:

- Cash crunches caused by preset interest payment deadlines can come at critical moments and cause owner/managers concern and sleepless nights.

- Management's time and focus can be easily diverted if cash flow strains are frequent or ill-controlled.

- Investment through debt can create undercapitalization with detrimental effects on the company.

- Collateral requirements by debt finance partners can prove constraining.

- Equity investors may be reluctant to commit initial or additional funds if management utilizes debt too readily.

- Debt financing investors tend to require better maintained financial records and performance ratios, including, but not limited to:

    Predetermined payable and receivable ratios.

    Constraints on the volume and aging of receivables.

    Inventory requirements adhered to and checked regularly.

    Net worth versus current assets guidelines at or better than market averages.

Equity Financing Is the Usual Route

Equity financing is the route most commonly selected, no matter the structural choice. It is a widely held belief among capital sources that over 80 percent of the funds raised for privately held enterprises is in the form of equity.

Whether or not this is always the best choice is questionable. Far too often entrepreneurs lament their choice too late. While equity is less demanding in many ways, its ultimate cost in terms of control of day-to-day decisions as well as the rewards to the original founders can be high.

It is easy to understand why most companies choose to sell equity in their organization. The terms are more flexible and the investors who back this form of investment appear on the surface to be less immediately demanding.

Advantages of Equity Financing

Other major advantages of equity investment include the following:

- Cash flow can be retained for growth in the business.
- Few equity investors demand immediate results.
- At least in the early stages, setbacks and unanticipated delays are not cause for concern on the part of most equity participants.
- Equity participation builds the balance sheet.
- Vendors, bankers, customers, employees, and existing partners all experience a higher degree of confidence when additional equity capital is infused into the entity.
- Equity infusion allows for greater management flexibility and choices.
- Equity infusion creates better opportunity for acquisitions and mergers to more readily build the organization.

Disadvantages of Equity Financing

The downside of equity structuring is that you are giving up a piece of the action. Once that is done, under most circumstances, you will not or cannot get it back. That is the major drawback. Equity participants are with you for the life of the organization or until either you or they bail through an exit strategy.

Choosing to sell a part of yourself along with a part of your "baby" brings new participants (with their own vested interest) to the organization. Like it or not, equity participants begin to think almost immediately of the entity as "theirs." This often does not sit well with entrepreneurs. It is still a fact of entrepreneurial and/or intrapreneurial life when capital has exchanged hands.

With each new equity partner you acquire, the entire organization takes on a slightly different hue and shape. Their input, overtly or covertly, will begin from the moment their cash is in your account. They expect to be heard, acknowledged, and have actions taken on their recommendations.

Perhaps no message should be clearer. Virtually all equity participants will want to put some form of their own stamp on your decision making and the end results. This is one of the most compelling reasons to get to know them and let them get to know you before you accept their participation. Remember this:

You are buying them and their money even though you think they are buying you. It is actually a mutual purchase opportunity.

The primary difference between the debt and the equity investors is that one has a definite time period before the relationship expires; the other will be with you as long as the party lasts, unless given an opportunity for early exit.

At this point some key members of the management/decision-making team, just like yours, may promote bringing the money in through debt while others like the idea of equity far more. Remember, combinations can and do work.

A/B Offering: Combination of Debt and Equity

A side-by-side combination opportunity of debt and equity simultaneously is known as an A/B offering. One of the other widely used combinations is the convertible debt or convertible preferred stock offering. In the latter two the investor begins as a debt (or quas-debt, which is what preferred stock is) holder, with rights under certain guidelines and within restricted time periods to change his or her position to that of an equity participant.

There are ways to determine which type of investment would be best for you. The following guidelines are more than theory. Through my own experience I have found that any application of textbook philosophy needs to be perfected in the operating world. Thus, learning these textbook applications enhances your education. Customizing based on this knowledge and your own experience will result in better decisions.

So, let's say at this point that you prefer the general idea of debt; your potential partner is thinking equity. So far, the advisors on the investors' side are mute on the issue. There is more to the decision than what type they each feel comfortable pursuing.

SIX WAYS TO SPEND FUNDS

Because there are only six possible ways *any* organization can spend money, applying type to use is relatively simple. The interesting thing in the real world is that so few people and organizations take the time to align utilization with type of investment sought. It is both interesting and sad; sad, because closer alignment can make a world of difference when the time for sharing rewards comes.

Working Capital

The first area in which the newly birthed business entity will spend funds is for working capital—the money needed to run day-to-day operations. Working capital includes everything from the paper clips on the supply list to the salary or draw of the managers. Operating capital is always a requirement at every stage of the business development. Until the formalization of the new organization, these operating expenses are borne by the founders.

The most effective type of financing for working capital, when the financing is sought from outside the organization's internally generated cash flow, is in the form of debt. For most organizations, including our hypothetical one here, this should be a one-time request. Once the enterprise is under way, the cash required to operate and carry the monthly overhead should be internally generated.

Should you find after the first year that this is not the case (unless yours is an entirely R&D operation), you are probably sinking rapidly into substantial debt. If so, reassess the viability of the business.

Interest on acquired debt becomes included in the working capital budget. The principal of the debt may also be amortized and included in the working capital budget. Amortizing the debt is the most attractive way to approach repayment. It results in three things:

1. Your company does not get strung out with a large balloon payment facing you at what may be an extraordinarily bad time.
2. You and the management team have a more realistic perspective on the cost of funds with which you are operating (a greater appreciation for what it takes in real time with all resources to get the monkey off your back).
3. You are likely to get the approval of both potential and existing equity investors.

Capital Equipment

The second way in which organizations spend their capital is for equipment to run the organization. This ranges all the way from the phones and faxes to the operating machinery in the warehouse. Known as capital equipment in the parlance of the accounting world, these are the physical tools of your trade.

This type of expenditure can be best accomplished with debt. Because different equipment is needed at different stages of growth, separate funding for large capital equipment purchases can be independently financed. Leasing is the leading form of acquisition of the equipment needed for most businesses.

Another reason that debt is more attractive than equity to finance this type of expenditure is that technology changes create capital equipment obsolescence quickly. Being able to trade in or trade up in such a rapidly changing technological environment keeps your costs in line with your competitive performance.

Capital for Acquisitions

The third way in which funds are spent is to expand the growth or market share of the business through acquisitions. Acquisitions are the best means by which to quickly create greater corporate viability, stability, and cash flow. All, when done well, lead to greater success for the organization.

Acquisitions can be done either through debt or equity, or some combination, as discussed previously. Equity is usually the best choice. Whether debt or equity is a better alternative can best be answered once you determine the major benefits of the acquisition beforehand. The strategy behind the proposed acquisition will dictate the best alternative on how to finance it.

These are the primary questions to ponder before launching the acquisition and the hunt for the capital to finance it:

- Is the acquisition being accomplished for survival or for enhancement of the market position and growth of the company?
- Is this acquisition positioning the existing entity to garner greater market share or to reduce costs (i.e., production, staffing, distribution, marketing)?
- Will this acquisition extend or expand the craft, technology, or market position (real or perceived) of the company?
- Through acquiring the target organization, will the resulting combination allow you to do things better or to do better things?
- Will this acquisition bring about a culture creation or a culture clash?

The answers to these questions will help set the stage for the best type of financing for the acquisition. If the results are anticipated to yield virtually immediate or near-term results, debt can be considered. If, as more likely the case, the results are anticipated to be longer term in nature, equity is the best choice for new funds.

Seed Capital

The fourth way in which organizations divest themselves of funds is in the area defined as seed capital expenditures.

All new and existing businesses need seed money, which is distinct and separate from R&D funding. The first is used to investigate whether or not a new business venture is even feasible and then if it is viable. The latter is used to further develop those products and services that pass the feasibility test.

In widespread usage of the term, seed capital is the money necessary to begin an endeavor. For purposes of allocating funds, the definition is expanded. Seed money is what is needed to investigate the viability of a business or its expansion.

Seed capital should be funded with equity participation. In the case of most new entrepreneurial businesses, this is the founders' personal contributions, other than their time and energy. It is for this, more than the ideas themselves, that they are entitled to equity participation throughout the organization's life.

Funding seed money is risky business. There is no cash flow to be had during the investigative process. It is impossible to pay back a financing source from the results of spending the money in this fashion.

Those who fund this level or type of need generally get a disproportionate share of the ultimate results. Because there may never be any results, the cost of funding from outside sources for this type of expense is the highest of all.

Once you are ready for the developmental, or second, tier of risk capital, you are beyond the investigative period covered by seed capital needs. While growing the business, you may need seed capital again, and its use should be clearly allocated to the viability investigation of a new product, service, or delivery development.

Capital for Research and Development

In the fifth area, R&D, either debt or equity will work. It depends on the stage at which the work is being accomplished and what the anticipated turn time is for results to be generated. There is short-term development and there is long-term research.

A good general guideline is to consider that the longer it will take to get results from the endeavor, the further you should move away from debt funding toward equity funding. Debt nearly always has a shorter fuse and demands some cash flow. Thus, only short-term cash genera-tion can satisfy its requirements.

In most cases today R&D is a significant percentage of the overall operating budget. Allocating between 20 and 60 percent of the total operating budget today to R&D is normal, depending on the industry and the accelerated rate of technological change. It usually takes months, if not years, before results can be achieved and be measurable.

On the other hand, there may be individual projects in your R&D division that will generate short-term profitability and lend themselves to debt financing. You must be the judge.

R&D in many cases is one of the best uses of funds for a debt-to-equity type of funding. Particularly attractive for funding R&D is convertible preferred stock. Preferred stock is one of those financial animals that can transform when and if the circumstances are right. There is a strong case to be made for considering that some portion of any research budget be funded in this manner.

Capital for Marketing

The sixth, and last, area in which funds get absorbed is marketing and advertising. This is the most overused and overrated use of funds for many entrepreneurial (and intrapreneurial) undertakings.

Hard (real cash) dollars are often expended for these corporate needs when soft dollars (alliances, networking, trade-offs) could be utilized more effectively. The more hard cash allocated to this type of expense, the greater is the need for overall funding of the operation. Establishing partnerships and/or sharing arrangements to create sales and distribution is one of the best solutions to achieving desired results better and faster.

In many business plans the founders have the percentage of the budget allocated for marketing and advertising at the level that should be set aside for R&D and vice versa. Big mistake! Bootstrapping in this area can really pay off for the astute business owner/leader. Because most companies fund their marketing and advertising with equity, they a tend to give up more than they should to equity partners.

You will utilize both debt and equity in building your company because you will need it now, two years from now, and five years from now. How much you need depends on the budget for each phase required to build the company. Funds will be required for further developing of the patented product, establishing manufacturing, creating the distribution channels, opening up and building sales, and creating a management team to take the operation from inception to established growth.

THE CRITICAL ELEMENT OF TIMING

Some funds will be needed immediately; some as sales require. Thus, the next issue we address is timing. Timing the investment to your actual need for the funds is one thing. Another is the timing of the sources you most desire. Sometimes their timing and yours will not be in sync. As a result, you should be prepared with your backup plan.

Timing also often plays a part in deciding whether the corporate, partnership, or trust legal forms are best suited to the needs of the company, the players, and the evolution of the business cycles in which you participate.

Timing should be considered from the following perspectives:

1. *The time required from the point at which you begin the hunt for the money to the time you actually receive it.* Debt financing usually takes less time than equity financing. The documentation requirements alone are far less rigid and involved. Decision makers, both public and private, usually move faster on a debt decision and can access funds more readily.

   Whether seeking debt or equity, the more desperately you need the money, the weaker your negotiating position. The greater the money you seek, the better prepared your plan and team should be. You should also expect the hunt to take longer than you would like. Preparing for this puts you in a position of strength to negotiate the terms of the financing agreement. Venture capital groups, you will discover, often seek both debt and equity. Debt is attractive because of its shorter fuse on getting returns to them; equity gives them an ownership interest in the business.

2. *The time (effort) you and the team will be required to invest to make a presentation to the funding sources in a manner consistent with their requirements.* The amount of time you and the management team will invest in the capital hunt can become a sore point. If you expect at least one full-time founder, with others on call, to work *only* on capital sourcing, you will not be disappointed.

   If your business is of interest to highly sophisticated sources, it is going to take serious effort. Venture capital funds, corporate sponsors, and institutional investors all require much, both in print and in person. They are likely to demand more lengthy presentations, more of them, more legal and accounting work, and more members of your team being on call than with other funding entities.

   There is not necessarily a direct correlation between the number of dollars you seek and the amount of time to get them. More dollars may equate to one large player or a group of them (the "sophisticated" elephants) or many more smaller players. The amount of time it takes to get to these sources does not vary with the size of the request. If they are difficult and lengthy to get to for $1 million, they will be no less difficult if all you seek is $500,000.

Combinations of angel investors, private and personal funding sources, banks, and corporate partners are commonly the alternative. What they will require from you may end up being no less tedious; it will just be different for each entity.

3. *The time both you and the investors anticipate having their funds tied up in your operation.* Debt funding sources expect (and demand on occasion) their returns on schedule, as promised. They also anticipate that they will call the shots if the original terms are to be altered.

Generally, those investors who fund debt are more conservative and expect to move their investment within a relatively short time span (i.e., two to five years). Equity investors, especially those who lack substantial investment experience and late-stage venture capital sources, also may desire short holding periods. By anticipating the expected holding time for the investment, you can structure the investment exit differently from your own or from other investors.

For example, you may decide to utilize a one-year bank note to take care of capital equipment and working capital needs. Simultaneously, you may decide to sell shares in your organization to fund the set-up of manufacturing, procure distribution channels, and begin marketing/advertising. You may plan to offer a second round of equity participation a year later to further build distribution and sales and to retire any remaining balance of the bank note. Both rounds of participants in these equity offerings should anticipate that their funds will not be returned, or appreciation garnered, until a public offering is made (which may yet be years away).

4. *How flexible the potential funding sources will and can be on item number 3.* Funding flexibility is related to the depth of the source's pockets. Whether or not they will *choose* to be flexible is a question only if they have the capability to do so. When

future funding is required, as it is with all successful enterprises, the onus is on the organization to prove performance and reason for continued or renewed interest and possibilities, even when short of initial projections.

It is in the best interest of the organization to determine from the outset the depth of the pockets of every funding source. Whether their results are ahead of or behind projections, this is the best source to return to for additional funding.

5. *How many times you expect to "go to the well" for additional capital.* You can almost count on two rounds of financing within the first two years. The first round is seeking funding to carry the organization through the manufacturing setup and distribution building process, maintain one year of working capital, meet R&D needs, and make any contemplated acquisitions to more quickly build market strength. The second round should be to give the organization the boost it needs to get to the next level of market dominance and profitability.

As a result, perhaps the first round of equity will be completed as a convertible preferred and the second as a common stock offering.

6. *The time it will take to get the operation to a positive cash flow position that will relate to returns to the investors.* The longer it is going to take to create positive cash generation, the less likely it is that debt will work in any substantive way. Selling debt to investors without any cash generation between the time of investment and maturity is a very hard sell. Debt investors like regular reports of progress. Even more, they like regular, planned cash return. You may determine it will take a solid three years to bring the first round of products out to a wide enough market with the profit parameters that generate positive income *and* cash flow. If so, debt does not seem to be a viable choice.

This is an important part of the formula in determining whether to accept debt financing. In the case outlined here, there will be insufficient cash flow to maintain any but the most moderate level of debt. Thus, by now you should have decided to seek equity investment for all areas of expenditure other than for capital equipment.

CHOICE OF LEGAL STRUCTURE

Now that they have considered the type of investment structuring and the timing of capital needs, the team is ready to assess the legal entity or entities. Basically there are choices to be made between the various forms of legal ownership for businesses. The one frequently used by sole practitioners is that of the sole proprietorship. This is an attractive choice for many individual entrepreneurs, whether it be for full-time or part-time business endeavors.

Sole Proprietorships

A sole proprietorship is the simplest and easiest of all business forms. No special documentation is required. The entrepreneur just opens for business and begins. The most complicated it gets is filing a "DBA" (doing business as) form with the local county clerk's office in order to do business under a fictitious name.

Proprietorships are also attractive because the business itself is not taxed. Whether positive or negative income, the results pass through to the individual. This single taxation can become a competitive advantage.

There are two primary drawbacks to this form of legal formation: (1) the general liability of the proprietor should something go wrong and (2) the cumbersome nature of transferring the business. Only through gift, sale, or will at the time of death can the proprietorship transfer its ownership.

For any proprietor wishing to bring in another owner, the legal form automatically converts to a partnership at the time of expansion. This happens whether or not that is the intended result. The result of two or more joining to conduct business together is a general partnership.

General Partnerships

This voluntary association of two or more people can be on equal terms or otherwise, if written into a legal agreement. It can be started as simply and easily, without legal registration, as a sole proprietorship. Many partners, however, formalize the major aspects of their agreement, particularly questions regarding sharing of profits and losses, withdrawal of one or more of the parties, and incorporation of additional members.

Because partnerships don't pay taxes either, the advantage of single taxation is available for this form of legal ownership also. This is probably the general partnership's greatest advantage.

The major disadvantage is the general liability all partners face. They can be held individually liable for all debts and obligations of the business. Innocent partners can face the responsibility of paying for the incompetence or negligence of their partners. Such obligations may be met with business assets and also with personal assets of any of the partners.

Unless there are buy–sell agreements in place and/or agreements that allow for transfer of partners' interests in the event of divorce, disability, retirement, death, or plain desire for the resignation of particular individuals, the partnership is normally considered to be dissolved by law. There is no automatic process in any of these cases. It must be established by the group, whether at the outset or while operating the business.

Whenever a new partner is admitted, the terms of the partnership are usually altered. Agreements need to be amended. Management roles may change. Again, try to build in this kind of flexibility from the beginning and it will pay off in time and money saved.

Limited Partnerships

This form of legal ownership is a distinct legal entity created under state law. There may be one or more general partners and one or more limited partners. The general partner runs the show and takes on the liability. The limited partners often provide the capital to fuel the business. Their liability is limited to the amount of their invested capital.

The terms of the agreement between general and limited partners are defined by a limited partnership agreement. Generally, the limited partners are provided a priority return from the business profitability. The general partners are paid for their management time and expertise and have a subordinated share in the business profitability.

Again, this form of legal ownership allows for pass-through tax treatment of the income and loss of the operation. While in some states there are complicated steps to ensure this advantage, generally it is one of the major benefits of the limited partnership.

The primary advantage to the limited partners is the opportunity to invest in an attractive business opportunity without incurring the liability of their personal assets should something go wrong. The disadvantage is the legal restriction on their voice in the day-to-day operations of the business. The penalty for exceeding the limits set by the state in which the business is operated is to convert a limited partner into a general partner.

It is the general partner who makes all crucial decisions for the business, without access to the skills and input of the limited partners. That is the offset to their general liability.

In the 1980s, limited partnerships flourished, particularly in industries targeted for favorable tax treatment. After the tax law changes in the middle to late 80s, the public utilization of this structure lost favor, at least as far as the untrained eye could tell.

Behind the scenes, this form of capitalization has continued, virtually unabated, to be utilized for significant product and service development. Fortune 500 companies and small enterprises alike use this structure to take advantage of the favorable liability and tax treatment it offers.

Corporations

Corporations may either be S, C, or LLC. All have significant advantages as well as disadvantages. Corporations are the leading business form in the United States today.

Corporations are treated by law as separate and distinct entities from their owners. Owned by shareholders, but managed by directors and officers, owners are afforded the opportunity of owning and running a business without risking all their personal assets.

Because a unique and distinct entity is created under law, it has an indefinite and continuous life. This continuity can provide a sustainable competitive and financial advantage to the business. It also provides a means by which interest or shares can be transferred without special agreements between shareholders. Even for corporations not traded on a public market, this allows much greater freedom of transferability and assignability of their ownership interest.

One important characteristic of the corporation that provides great flexibility is the variety of tools available to customize ownership as well as management of the business. Equity participation may be either in the form of common, preferred, or convertible preferred stock. Debt can be either preferred (senior) or subordinated. Stock may or may not carry voting rights. Quorum and veto rights for management and directors can be set either high or low.

With all these positive characteristics, the trade-off is the tax position of the corporation. Because it is treated as a separate legal entity, it has its own tax imposed on its profitability before any distributions are made to shareholders. This means double taxation for the individual shareholders.

Choosing from among the S, C, and LLC should hinge on the complexity and overall objectives of the endeavor being launched. The potential of the organization (or the specific part of it that you are concerned with at the moment) to go to a broad market of public trading is another serious consideration. The objectives and exit strategies of the key founders, allied partners and/or corporations, managers, and significant investors also help determine the selection.

The S Corporation

The S Corporation is the limited solution to the double taxation problem. This form of legal ownership allows the corporation to elect to let earnings flow through to the shareholders. This allows single taxation, like that of proprietorships and partnerships.

To make things simple, most S corporations have only one owner or two related owners (typically husband and wife, or two generations of the same family). Usually they wish to conduct business in such a way as to maximize tax treatment of their income. The S structure allows the use of corporate titles, outward perception, and other corporate image benefits yet provides a single taxation on the year-end distribution of the profits. In many states the number of shareholders in S corporations is very limited, at the most 35.

As outside investors take part in the financing of the organization (become part of the 35 legally allowable shareholders), legal restrictions in addition to investor demand warrant a change to a more conventional corporate positioning. The tax benefits are, after all, one of the potential assets of the corporation. Thus, investors expect or demand that they be treated on the same footing as others when they become your equity partners.

The following are requirements of the S format that can restrict the operation and growth of the business:

- All shareholders must be U.S. citizens, residents of the United States, or some defined trusts. (Note: Corporations, partnerships, and many trusts *cannot* be shareholders.)
- There can be only one class of stock—common.
- There can be no more than a 79 percent interest in any subsidiary corporation.

- Shareholders who initially meet the criteria must continue to do so for the life of the corporation.
- There are limits on the use of debt to create a tax basis.
- There are prohibitions on special allocations of income.

Founders who agree they want a structure that is more amenable to outside investors and one that offers them greater flexibility usually decline to consider an S for themselves.

The C Corporation

Those organizations that include more than one owner and have the outlook to build a substantial business usually begin operations as C corporations. All states have C corporations. As stated above, this is the most widely used form of legal business ownership.

Many new corporations have been and continue to be incorporated in the states of Delaware and Nevada. These states are widely used, primarily for ease of process, reporting, and favorable tax and/or publicity purposes.

For sake of discussion here, let's say C corporations represent what the general public identifies as corporate structure. Such organizations are legally registered to do business within one or more states. Typically they have a corporate headquarters easily discernible and within the legal requirements for agent and place of legal process. Most have a board of directors, officers, employees, customers, vendors, and suppliers.

The greatest disadvantage of the C corporation is the double taxation of the business profitability. As a result, many business owners opting for this form of ownership make every effort to minimize the income of the business. Paying as much as possible in tax-deductible compensation is just one widely employed tactic. Another common practice is for the owner/shareholders to finance the business with debt they provide. The interest payments become a tax deduction and repayment of principal is tax free.

The growing concern about the overtaxation of corporations and growing global competition forced government bodies to consider alternative structures to create and sustain business growth. In the past two decades many state governments have been forced to consider ways of improving their economic environments. This has led to the business form that is rapidly becoming the form of choice for young businesses in these final years of the 20th century: the limited liability corporation.

Limited Liability Corporation (LLC)

The limited liability corporation was introduced to the United States by the state of Wyoming in 1977. Wyoming borrowed from foreign nations to create a new form that broke ground with existing legal business structures within the country. The state chose the name that, as of this printing, has been selected by 48 states.

The relatively sudden, rapid, and widespread popularity of the LLC arises from its advantages of partnership treatment within the confines of corporate perception.

The primary characteristics of the LLC are these:

- Limited liability (similar to that of corporate shareholders).

- Pass-through taxation (similar to that of proprietorships, partnerships, and S corporations).

- Existing businesses can in most cases convert without adverse tax treatment.

- No restrictions on permitted owners (similar to C corporations).

- No restrictions on active participation (unlike the closely monitored restrictions on the limited partners in limited partnerships).

- Flexibility of operation (similar to C corporations).

- Customization of the business operation works well whether the business is simple and small or complex and large.

LLCs can be established to pursue the same business opportunities as other forms of business enterprise (proprietorship, corporation, general and limited partnerships). Because this hybrid combines characteristics of both corporate and partnership law, it is relatively easy to understand.

One important addition, beyond the scope of this book, is the possible not-for-profit and "nonbusiness" purpose possibilities of the LLC. Because of the tax pass-through feature of the LLC, it may become the form of choice for the former. Until now, the only means by which nonprofits have been able to secure such tax treatment has been by utilizing the general partnership format. In the case of individual creation of an LLC, the liability issue may be one of the most attractive features for consideration. In either or both cases, you should consult your attorney and review the applicable state law.

With these choices now in mind, how will you structure your business? Will you choose debt or equity or some combination? Will you go first round debt and simultaneously launch the safari for equity partners?

Will you choose to remain a sole proprietor if you are in business alone? Will you bring in one or more partners to operate more or less on an equal basis? Will you go in search of limited partners, putting yourself in the general partner role? Will you choose to begin as an S corporation, limiting your number of shareholders? Will you stay with the traditional C corporate structure? Will you readily accept the new format of the LLC?

THE SAN FRANCISCO INVESTMENT BANKER

Recently during a lecture on capital formation I was delivering in San Francisco, I was in the midst of explaining the various types and forms of structure available for the capital infusion. I told the audience it was important to match the structure with utilization of the funds and the business objectives for the time period in which they would be spent.

Suddenly a man near the front of the room jumped up and shouted to his associate in the back of the room, "That's it! No wonder we couldn't get our deal off the ground for over a year!"

When he calmed down, he shared with all of us their struggle to fund their project. This experienced investment banker had spent over $100,000 of his own money to get the proper documentation and presentation packages in place to make his offering. Month after month had slipped by without funding. The investors just weren't buying the deal. By the time I saw the man and his partner at my presentation, a whole year had gone by literally without result. Things still looked bleak. That is why they were there. The investment banker and his business colleagues kept butting their heads into a stone wall.

After the lecture, we talked. I gave him some options to consider. I shared with him questions (the ones I have shared with you here) to ask of himself and his partner that were directly related to the structure of the business. I reminded them to take time to understand their reasons for choosing a particular form.

Six weeks later, he called my office and told me the good news. They had successfully funded their project in one month after changing their offerings along the lines I had suggested they investigate.

I congratulated him and told him to follow through and build a successful company.

You see, even veteran investment bankers with experience, savvy, and sophistication sometimes get confused about the most appropriate form of financial structuring.

FINANCING STRATEGIES NEED TO BE CUSTOMIZED

It would be great if I could provide you with a template that works every time, one on which you could just overlay your project and come up with the right financial structure. But it doesn't work that way. You cannot carbon copy financing strategies.

If finding the winning combination were simple, all the NFL teams would end up in the Super Bowl; every tennis player would win at Wimbledon; every college basketball team would go to the Final Four; every yachting crew would win the America's Cup races; and every pro golfer would win the green jacket at the Masters.

No. You have to do your own homework and figure out what will work for you in the particular situation you are in at the moment. You need to figure out what is appropriate for your special situation. Doing this is an art, not a science.

Yes, there are formulas, but the formulas lack one important ingredient—your personal thumbprint, emotions, dreams, goals, and personality. There is no one correct capital formation strategy and structure for your company. Over time there are likely to be many.

CHAPTER 6

Understanding Potential Investors' Perspectives

The top 1 percent of the households in America account for nearly 40 percent of the wealth. Traditional methods of marketing and selling as well as advertising, are often ineffective determinants of the patronage behavior of the affluent. The affluent respondents whom I have interviewed report that interpersonal endorsements were most influential in their decisions to patronize a variety of product and service providers.

Dr. Thomas J. Stanley
Author, "Networking with the
Affluent and Their Advisors"

You know, quite precisely by this time, *what* you want. You may assume the investors do, too. Sometimes they do. Sometimes they are waiting for you to tell them. The less sophisticated the potential investor, the more the latter will be true.

The more concrete and defined their own plan, the greater the possibility that the potential investors to whom you present your ideas will know whether or not your offering falls within the boundaries of their consideration.

The personality and decision-making characteristics of your potential investing partners are difficult to read. However, you can rely on two elements that will flavor any decision by *any* party to whom you present. These are the elements of greed and fear. All potential investors possess both, and both will ultimately play a part in their decision making.

There are times and ways to play to both. Your ability to read which is at work in potential investors will be extremely useful.

To hone your skills at reading these investors, from the moment you first encounter them through their investment in your company or project, there are a few rules to learn. The most important are the following:

1. *Determine in each circumstance if the potential investor is moved largely by greed or largely by fear.*

   Interestingly, even sophisticated venture capital sources and broker-dealer networks often have guidelines that have elements of flexibility. They (and any potential investor) may be largely oriented to those opportunities that spell instant success and phenomenal returns. On the other hand, certain potential sources usually are so fearful that they put up one hurdle after another, not only to you and other potential deals, but in their own minds as well.

   The best news for you is to realize that no one will ever act totally from a point of view of either greed or fear. There will be those times when the most fearful will take a leap of faith and invest. There will also be times when those who appear to be purely greedy will develop a soft spot and invest more humanely or for reasons out of their normal mode. Just remember, most investors will act "in" rather than "out" of their traditional character most of the time. That is why determining which of the extremes is their particular modus operandi is helpful.

Nonetheless, the times when they do act out of character are the holes in their net that may allow you to come swimming through, if you can read their hidden agendas as well as you can their exterior motives.

A word to the wise: Those hidden agendas often involve third parties not immediately or directly involved in your opportunity. There is little you can do about this, and you may not even be cognizant of the entities or their influence. Just be aware!

2. *Do your homework to understand who you are enticing to be your investing partner. This homework involves understanding as much as possible about them, including business and personal connections that may play a part either initially or eventually in their involvement with your offering.*

Lining up as many of the advantages as you can on your side is good business. The way you do that, giving yourself the *unfair advantage,* is to know more about them than they know about you. This means understanding their background, their motivations for business decisions, their meaningful relationships and the import of each to their business and personal performance, and how they act out their priority values.

The good news is that by asking questions and by doing your homework by checking on their background, preferences, relationships, and the like, you will make a wiser choice. The bad news is that in the early stages of virtually any relationship it is almost impossible to determine how people will react in a given situation. That's life.

Even if you approach only family and friends, or funding sources close to home and intertwined in the operation of your organization, asking for and receiving investment capital is business with a capital B. People and companies take money seriously.

Remember the adage "Fools rush in where angels fear to tread." At times you may lose your head and rush forth with such excitement and enthusiasm that you overlook this step. When that happens, hope you are walking with angels. Doing your homework is one of the most important rules of business, easy to overlook in one's exuberance.

3. *Take the time to get to know as well as you possibly can the people you are asking to be part of your life as your investing partners.*

Accepting your funding partners is much like entering into a marriage. Once you tie the knot (sign the contract) there is no easy way out.

Another consideration is that this marriage is more likely than not to run into some choppy waters. Add to that the high probability that one or the other of you will be disappointed in how things go and what ultimately transpires and you will understand much better the nature of the relationship into which you are entering.

The termination or disintegration of the relationship is often expensive. And the costs are not always only monetary.

You should want to create a good relationship with your funding sources. Ultimately, this is something you are doing not just for the funding source, but also for yourself.

Good relationships are energizing; bad ones exhausting, frustrating, and potentially debilitating. You do yourself, your entire team, *and* the funding source a major favor by thinking through their acceptance and understanding at least the surface risks of the relationship from the beginning.

To determine their perspective and expectations, all you need do is *ask!* I suggest once you know this source has a serious interest in playing in your sandbox that you turn the tables and interview them. Use hypothetical questions relative to their expectations, timelines, and possible reactions to future setbacks and disappointments that might occur. Then gauge their response relative to your own. See how good the match is or is not before going to the next level.

Now that you know the rules that absolutely should not be broken in *any* circumstance when you pursue capital for your company or project, let me share some questions I have developed over the years to help entrepreneurs find and select which partners suit them and their circumstances best.

FIVE TYPES OF QUESTIONS TO ASK IN THE SEARCH FOR THE RIGHT INVESTING PARTNER

The following five areas of questioning have proven to be invaluable in selecting the right investment partners. You need information on your investing partners' expectations regarding communication, cash flow to them, dealing with setbacks and/or failure, solutions they would most support, and how they would handle higher than anticipated success.

The following specific questions are a beginning. Customize your own list by adding other key questions that you develop throughout your money hunt. Asking is the only way to get a clear picture of the person or entity to whom you are about to be aligned and the only way to make a rational decision on whether to say yes or no to the capital they offer.

1. *a.* What frequency of communication from me (our organization) do you want?

    b. Must it be me or does it matter *who* your contact person is?

    c. What do you consider totally *un*acceptable communication (style, time of call, frequency, etc.)?

2. *a.* Should cash dividends or return be made at the sacrifice of honest communication?

    b. In *your* opinion, when should dividends not be made?

3. *a.* How would you propose I deal with the bad and the ugly news that could affect the company and, consequently, your capital investment?

    b. What is your *need to know quotient* (about daily trials and tribulations, potentially serious or hazardous situations, problems in general)?

4. *a.* When specifically financial problems arise, there are only a handful of solutions for any business. Which are the ones and under what circumstances would you recommend as our primary considerations?

    b. If additional investment is called for, and it is voluntary, would you have the capability to participate? What would be your criteria to do so? And would you?

5. In the event of excess cash flow generated in the company, would you "make a higher, special distribution to yourself" or "invest substantially all of the excess to expand the company's growth"?

All of this is leading to creating the relationship you want over time with each selected investor. My advice is to have a game plan for each and every investor that comes on board.

Just remember, it is often much easier to accept an investor than to oust one. Once involved in the investment, the guidelines for removal are burdensome. This can come back to bite you if you do not consider it seriously *before* accepting the relationship.

Substitution provisions and lack of ready transferability are often fundamental to the underpinnings of any private investment offering. You must understand what happens in the event of an investor's death, permanent disability, or hardship. The rules vary among states and among particular legal structuring entities (i.e., limited partnership, C corporations, business trusts, limited liability corporations).

With that said, it is good to remember that all investing partners will be slightly different, with a slightly different focus. You are the one to create, nourish, and build on the initial relationship you have with each to bring about a cohesive, cooperative, and supporting investor group.

The investors, once on board, are now part of the organization. Your outlook should be to make that part of the organism (the investor group) functional, supportive yet nonobtrusive, and essentially satisfied.

When we talk about a game plan that differs for each investor, we must consider the rules and regulations that legally govern this to some extent. No special favors or deals can be cut with one investor over another. Nor can official communications be sent to only screened or hand-selected investors.

Under the securities rules, you are required (or, in the case of private offerings, advised) to communicate with them a minimum number of times per year. In general, you should consider at least quarterly communication, with an annual review and forecast.

The terms of your original documentation in accepting investors should set the guidelines for each of the five areas we discussed earlier— all relative to setting investor expectations. Check with your attorney to be sure you will be in compliance with the applicable laws governing your organization.

Be sure you set your own communication requirements very carefully, considering the staffing and time requirements to meet these objectives. You *must* act within the legal framework of your particular state; if you choose to do more (or to exceed expectations), be sure you will be able to follow through for the life of the project or company. It is good business to exceed the legal guidelines in this area; it just takes more in terms of time and resources to carry it out.

SCOUTING FOR THE "IDEAL" INVESTOR

While the "ideal" investor from your point of view may not exist, with careful scouting you can find those that come very close. Some characteristics that are worth searching for are these:

- Mutual care and respect for one another, for one another's position, expectations, responsibilities, demands, and ultimate desire for the endeavor.
- Sharing a common sense of mission and purpose.
- Developing a sense of adventure in the possibilities for the endeavor and bringing all resources available from the parties to bear on the growth and health of the organization.
- Both sides maintaining high self-esteem, flexibility, and resilience, to deal with changing situations, setbacks, and outside influences with integrity.

There are three traits in my experience that identify the "ideal" investor. These are:

interested, committed, experienced.

The ideal investor you should seek is one who believes in both you and your business, but is realistic in his assessment. The investors should be as committed to your success as you are. They should be ready and able to assist you in achieving that success with any network or resources available to them. They should offer you a viable sounding board.

Certain legal structures, such as those of limited partnerships and certain limited liability corporations, do not allow investing partners to take a role in the actual management of the business or project. Encouragement, input, and contacts to help you grow the business, however, are not only allowed but also should be encouraged.

The better you know and understand the prior experience of your investors, how they responded to developing situations, and how they ultimately fared, the better prepared you will be to answer their concerns and deal realistically with their expectations. This knowledge can also help you avoid pitfalls and learn the best means of communication. Without this knowledge many business owners/leaders have responded to developing situations with communications that trigger buried emotions and reactions from their investors.

One thing that does not necessarily make for an "ideal" investor is passivity.

You might think that having an investing partner who simply hands over funds and waits quietly in the wings, without comment on your progress or success, is just what you want. Not necessarily so. Investors who are as passive as this usually harbor their own priorities and perceptions, which, left unaddressed, may lead to difficulty in the sequence of future fundings and other development.

Passivity does not necessarily mean approval. While some element of "wait and see" is part of nearly all investors, the truly interested ones are highly unlikely to maintain silence as you proceed.

FIVE CATEGORIES OF INVESTOR TYPES

Investors tend to fall into one of five categories. This includes both individuals and groups. The lead investor and/or the contact person for a group will usually demonstrate certain qualities that define himself and, to the extent that he adequately represents the group, the investors behind the curtains.

Nervous Investors

The first category is that of *nervous investors*. These investors usually have expectations of their own making, not what you tell them. Their expectations are usually based on criteria separate from the terms actually defined in your offering. While every category of investor bases certain expectations on their own past experience, nervous investors fall back into the past or rely on old habit patterns far more than any other classification. Within those you will categorize as nervous, there are three designations.

The first example of nervous investors are those who have little or no experience in investing in either the discipline your business represents and/or in the structure and style of the offering. This group will require maximum hand-holding to understand virtually every little move and/or requirement of the structure of the capital itself.

The second example of nervous investors are those who either have prior experience investing in a business similar to your own or in the type of structure you have selected. This group has tasted some success in their past experience but has also endured some difficult moments, even losses, from prior investments.

They will be constantly on the lookout for tell-tale signs similar to their previous experience that tell them they may be in trouble. The good news about this group is that if it is *you* that lacks certain experience, they can provide you an early warning sign of something that may be going off course. The bad news, of course, is that every little hiccup that even remotely looks like a problem from the past will cause them concern that they will voice.

The third example of nervous investors are those who should have left their money in either their pockets or bank accounts. They are the ones who have stretched beyond their means to participate in your game.

Their financial commitment to you exceeds their flexibility in either their own personal or professional lives and often will create a strain in that arena that may create a pressure point. They mean well. They understand and buy your dream and ability to do it. They just don't have much staying power.

This is the group that either financially or emotionally (or both) cannot afford to lose their investment. Often, this group includes family members and friends. You may know beforehand that they are likely to fall into this category.

Sometimes you can be creative in allowing them to participate in some other way. Often it appears you are trying to keep them from participating in a lucrative bonanza if you turn them down. This is a tricky one.

The better you understand that only those who can really afford total loss are those you should accept as investing partners, the less likely you will be to accept either individuals or groups for whom the financial risk is inappropriate either to their financial status or emotional/psychological response.

Remember, *all* investors will be nervous to one degree or another. The higher the level of nervousness (at least that which you can observe), the more grief you can usually anticipate.

Let me share a little secret. *The better you get at assessing the risk-tolerance of any potential investor, the better you will get at reading the nervous or risk-averse level of all people with whom you are dealing, including your own management team members as well as yourself. You become aware of times in which you are stretching beyond the limits of your own and your team's collective comfort level. Tracking this will allow you to develop a "gut feel" of how nervous different decisions and their potential outcomes make you.*

Backseat Driver Investors

The second type of investor is the one who wants to have input into the business decisions but does not want to be part of the day-to-day work required of the management team. We will call this group the *backseat drivers.*

Unlike the nervous investors, who are more typically quiet and keep their concerns to themselves until they finally reach the point of explosion, backseat drivers rarely keep their thoughts to themselves. As a result, they can help you achieve good, open communication with all of the investors *or* they can create dissension and unrest because they are often perceived by others to be in a position of strength within the organization. If their position is contrary to yours, you will be forced to take a strong stance with them.

This type of investor needs to be identified quickly and harnessed by an appropriate manager and/or director to maximize the benefit she can bring while minimizing the damage she can create. While it is critical that you "read" this type of investor as soon as possible, even more important is that you enroll her as part of a unified front.

Acknowledge their strengths and show that you welcome their input but determine what you most want from them. These particular investors are quite real and often found in fast-growing entrepreneurial companies.

Initially, some start slowly and are hard to detect. Others are clear from the outset that their money is only one of the tools they will provide you.

The first example of backseat drivers are those whose own prior experience in the corporate or business world fell short of what they wanted to accomplish. Now, through investment and involvement with you and your group, they may have a second chance to prove their theories or prowess.

A second example are those whose own success has led them to relive, albeit vicariously, the thrill and challenge once again. They want to stay close to the action and give you their input as much as you are willing to take it. Beneath their exterior beats the heart of a quarterback or fullback dying to get back into the game. They will definitely meet the criteria of believing in the product, the marketplace, and the potential of the endeavor. Often they just feel they could do the job better, faster, with greater aplomb than perhaps you do. So they will not be shy in sharing their opinions.

Investors in this category are often slightly older, perhaps a little worn around the edges. Investors who lack prior experience tend to be more nervous, but they don't have the answers to the problems that surface. This backseat drivers group, on the other hand, always has at least one solution ready, often many. They hope you will take their advice before the final decision is made rather than after.

Whatever experience they bring to the table, one thing is for certain: *They have been there and done that.* And wherever "there" has been and whatever "that" was, it has some bearing on what you and the company are currently experiencing or will go through.

The good news about this group is that they tend to bring in a wealth of contacts from their network. The bad news is that they will attempt to foist on you "experts" whose style, philosophy, conduct, and agenda are more in alignment with the introducing investor than with your own. Some of them will be great, and others, as in all things, will not be the right mix.

Three observances about backseat drivers follow:

1. Because their "armchair" approach means they will give you input frequently, there can be a tendency to treat them much like the little boy who cried wolf too often. Their input can be highly valuable. Check it out before disregarding it.

2. When this investor is treated with respect, courtesy, and a fair hearing, this is the investor who will go to the wall for you. Because they can and do find other valuable players to help fill gaps in the organization, they take a far more personal interest in growing the business rather than merely in the financial outcome. Your biggest fan club will be made up of investors in this group. I suggest you pay close attention to them. If you lose their support and confidence, something is probably seriously off track.

3. Clearly hear them out. Acknowledge their invaluable input, perhaps make adjustments that reflect some element of their ideas and input, and forge ahead. In most circumstances, the investors are limited by the legal structure as to their direct involvement in your company. Your own strength, discipline, and leadership will be honed with their input and support.

Investors Who Like Their Hands Held

The third type of investor are the ones who like to have their hands held and receive "strokes" from you and other members of the management team. (These are not nervous investors, they just want attention.) They want to hear from you relatively frequently, although it is the quality not the quantity of communication that is important to them. We will call them the ego gratification investors.

This is the group that most enjoys the latest "news flashes" and up-to-date information on minutia. Often entrepreneurs and upper management people are so busy in their daily progress that this investor can be an irritant. Getting someone in your organization to be the liaison to these investors is a very good move, as soon as you can afford the position.

Often this type of investor is seeking something more from the investment than merely financial reward. They seek gratification in knowing they are participating in a growing, exciting endeavor. They may be seeking assurance of their financial acumen and more. Their ego is often integrally related to the investment and/or association with you, the management team, the directors, and other sophisticated or highly regarded investors.

The psychological, social, or emotional payoff potential of the investment is nearly as important to these "handholding investors" as the financial one. Just remember, they may talk up these other sides, but, ultimately, they put real value on the financial reward. In fact, this group is usually the one to most criticize underperformance and undervalue overperformance. Because their egos are caught up in their investment, they will tend to take credit for the positives and hold you personally responsible for any setbacks.

The "why" of their initial investment has as much to do with them, personally, as it does with you and the offering. They want something else from the investment—until the time comes for payback. Your job (in their eyes) is to keep them happy on the other levels until that day comes. Of all investors, this is the one who least accepts setbacks and failure.

Investors with a Hidden Agenda

The fourth type of investor is the one who has other vested interests in the growth and success of your venture. We will call this investor the *hidden agenda* investor.

Other opportunities, connections, or developments that have a serendipitous effect on other holdings or connections these investors have often leads them to invest in your enterprise.

The first example of such an investor is one who may be developing a new product or process or testing a newly devised distribution or sales idea. By investing through the venue of your product or company, the investor determines this may be the least costly way to achieve breakthroughs for his existing business.

Another example of such an investor is one who anticipates that your organization's research and development will lead to opportunities for other associations she is affiliated with.

These investors also may be seeking strategic partnering or alliances with other groups they are engaged with or they may be seeking a potential new division for their larger corporation.

By investing in an entrepreneurial endeavor that allows explosive opportunity with relatively small amounts of capital infusion, such investors can test markets, products, services, delivery systems, and people with a modicum of risk. In other words, such investors can test the waters before committing themselves to a truly significant time and capital decision.

Investors who fall into this category rarely do so casually. Usually they are the most familiar with your particular business and its opportunities. Because they are most familiar with the industry, the technology, or the market you are addressing, they will do their homework well to understand the role and background of each and every major participant in the operation.

Their own backgrounds, current positions, interest in the technology or other innovative features of your organization dictate a high level of interest in your progress (one of the elements of the "ideal" investor). The process of your progress may be of as much interest to them, or even more, than the outcomes. Keep this in mind.

Often, hidden agenda investors may already have some tie to your operation. Corporate investors tend to fall into this category.

You may think you know what their ulterior motives are. What you are developing may well feel like a solid fit for their organization later, when it is more fully developed and the bugs are few and far between. There is often more than that, more than immediately meets the eye.

Of all investors, it will be these who will be most keenly alert to possible expansion opportunities as they involve other businesses, lateral moves, or unusual associations (again, another element of the "ideal" investor—experience).

Strategic partnering allows growth and/or savings that can benefit existing as well as future financial investment partners, customers, and the marketplace. They will understand that most readily and be won over to your thinking more rapidly than investors in either the nervous or ego categories will be. That is, if it is not in conflict with the agenda that may be hidden from your view.

So long as their agenda does not conflict with the philosophy, direction, and development of your enterprise, these investors will be invaluable resources to you. When and if a conflict arises, you are often the last to know. Stay alert to possible collisions by updating your knowledge of your investors as time marches on in your own development.

The Investor Closest to Your Ideal

The fifth type of investor is the one *you* choose who is closest to your own ideal, whatever that may be. Earlier in this chapter I shared three characteristics that I believe help define the best investors. But there certainly are other characteristics to be prized in your investing partners. Take time to think about which qualities and characteristics you rate the highest.

As you establish your own "ideal" criteria, keep in mind that setting expectations, yours and theirs, from the beginning of the relationship is important. To help you get started in this process, I offer the following thought-provoking questions for you to ask yourself before you select.

- Which character qualities would you like exemplified in your investors?
- How will you handle investors whose personalities and/or perspectives differ from your own?
- Does your offering attract all types of investors or one in particular?
- Are you discriminating or will you accept whoever shows up?
- What role, other than their money, do you want from your investors?
- What are you offering them, other than a return on their investment, that satisfies a need or desire they have?

I hope you now have a better idea of who you are looking for. Ideally, you will satisfy yourself with *who* you really want, not just pander to any money source that walks in the door. With this clearer picture in mind of what your "ideal" funding source looks like, now it is time to review where you can find it.

CHAPTER 7

Finding the Appropriate Investors

It is critical for young, fast-growth companies to find investors who are truly partners in the best sense of the word. You see, investors don't bring only money to the party. If you enroll them in your dream, your vision, they can be a most valuable source of contacts, potential strategic alliances, customers, vendors, distributors, and other funding sources. The right investor can be your best supporter and biggest promoter. And, if invited and encouraged, they can also help you make some very major deals.

Dan Stephenson
Founder and master developer
Temecula
(Rancho, California)

Now that you know who you are looking for in the ideal (or at least appropriate or acceptable) partner, how do you find that investor?

Before you dash off to New York, Los Angeles, or the other meccas of available entrepreneurial capital for meetings with the top investment banking and venture capital funds, take a moment to consider other sources.

LOOKING CLOSE TO HOME

Investors who are close to home are those most likely to fund critical early rounds. They are defined in three ways: (1) those close to you and your key team members in your personal relationships, (2) those close to you in a professional sense, and (3) those close to you geographically, whether known to you personally or not.

Because seed capital (the money required to test the viability of an idea and necessary for the launch of the business) is so difficult to come by, it is imperative that you not overlook any source that falls close to home. Unsophisticated and professional investors alike tend to invest in companies within reasonable travel distance from them (approximately 300 to 500 miles).

Thus, the following are all designated as close to home sources:

1. Current and past customers of the business being developed or expanded. It also includes past customers of all members of the management team as well as contacts of your consultants.
2. Current and past vendors; suppliers; distributors; marketing and advertising contacts; banking, accounting, legal, and other professional service contacts.
3. Current and past contacts through educational, social, political, economic, and other associations.
4. Current and past competitors.

Close to Home Sources for Existing Corporations

In the case of growing or large organizations developing new products and services, looking for funding from sources close to home should be done with two perspectives. The first is to look internally within the organization. The second is to pursue outside funding in the categories listed above, with emphasis on categories 1 and 2.

For example, pursuing internal funding means talking to other divisions and departments to uncover potential funds. You may find funds previously earmarked for other project developments that may now be sitting on a shelf or abandoned.

You will be "selling" your idea in much the same way as you would in searching for outside capital. By considering your sister division as a potential partner rather than as a competitor, you may create a strong bond while simultaneously finding the funding you desire. Answer the question of "what's in it for them?" just as you would any outside source.

Because of your position as a division of a larger entity, searching for external close to home sources takes on a different tone than if you are an independent entrepreneurial organization. It is likely that such a funding source has an even greater vested interest in what you are doing and has the capacity and the desire (sometimes) to become a strategic partner.

When such funding is secured, often totally new structures are devised. New corporations or partnerships are formed, or joint ventures between partners are put in place. Candidates for such investment/alliance can be horizontal or vertical. At times they may also be purely financial.

Witness the recent developments between Microsoft and America Online (AOL) or Netscape with CompuServe. Investment and partnering is a growing phenomenon for successful businesses today.

Let's review the process of looking for close to home funds recently undertaken by a young sandal company formed in Hawaii. Its experiences are shared with numerous start-up enterprises around the globe. Perhaps you will learn a few of the "dos" and "don'ts" that may apply to your own situation.

THE STORY OF THE OUTSIDERS OF HAWAII

The two young surfers got their start operating from a kiosk in Lahaina, Maui. They realized the sandals they were selling had a greater appeal and potential than most of the competition. They were not so unusual in design or material. They simply fit more people, of all ages and both sexes, better. Their customers raved about the feel and the fact that, even with considerable wear, they did not pick up the odor most other sandals did. Those were the two distinct advantages of the product—fit and nonretention of odor.

This, they determined, would be their avenue to fame and fortune, while allowing them to create something in alignment with their shared philosophies.

The opportunity to create something that investors and customers alike enjoyed and could actively participate in was one they could not pass up. Here was their chance to do something they and most of their surfing colleagues knew something about; it was a fun product and there was the potential to develop an entire line of related products; they could create events, especially in Hawaii, that could feature their wares; and they could go after an expanded base of participants, much like Ben & Jerry's had. What could go wrong?

With only meager personal resources but a ton of heart and determination, they became sponges for information relative to the manufacture, distribution, market appeal, and niche marketing strategies of successful companies. In other words, they had much more time than they did money and they invested it wisely.

As with most first-time entrepreneurs, their first stop was family and friends. (Close to home!) With enough funding in hand to get started, they decided to maximize their resources by keeping the business going at its existing level while they invested their own time to bone up on the people and approaches to best help them get the sophisticated, "serious" capital to take their idea to the big time.

This meant spending some of that money to attend conferences, both local and out of state. The intent was twofold: (1) to learn something about the various business aspects of running a successful enterprise and (2) to find potential funding sources, corporate partners, management additions, and customers.

In undertaking this process, especially once they went beyond those close to home with whom they had a relationship, they found themselves challenged to stay in alignment with their own integrity and dream. Not wanting to sell out too early with a dream clearly destined to be a winner, they decided, after just a few short weeks, to retrench and go in search of what they needed closer to home. They began a more intensive search back to the basics for both team members for management and for investing sources familiar either with them or the industry or who supported Hawaiian entrepreneurial development.

Their next round of funding came from some of their very first employees, mentors, and former business associates. Their enthusiasm was contagious. Like a magnet, their ideas, combined with their character and grit, brought the resources to them.

They opened doors to potential distributors, investors, and key retail partners through sheer chutzpah (and some key introductions) and leveraged their next funding from maximizing the resources with which they began and those uncovered once they got very serious about lifting all the rocks in their own backyard. Not until they reached this point did they begin to go beyond this close to home stage.

While in many start-up companies getting to the first stage of outside financing can easily take 6 to 12 months or more, in their case it took only 3.

THE NEXT STEP

Once you have exhausted your direct appeal to all those you and all team members can identify as close to home, the next best option is to network through professional service providers. While private funding sources (frequently referred to as angels) can at times be found through print resources or even on the Internet, it is far more likely you will find them through serious networking.

You should not overlook the print resources, however. The major publications that focus on entrepreneurial issues run quarterly or semi-annual updates of those sources that are at least semipublicly known. These publications include *Success, Inc., Entrepreneur, Forbes,* and *Black Enterprise,* to name a few.

But networking with real, live humans is far more likely to pay off with the capital you seek. Some of the best people with whom to begin include business lawyers who specialize in start-ups and/or initial public offerings (IPOs), accountants (pay particular attention to Big Six firms), financial planners and brokers, and business brokers.

If you can afford or can negotiate reasonable fees (that may be an interesting undertaking in itself) with one of the Big Six accounting firms, they can be worth their weight in gold. The same can be said of securing corporate and securities legal assistance.

Now, getting a professional you can talk to—*really* talk to—is the key. One who understands you and your business and what you want to accomplish is the ideal you should seek. Again, it is a difficult but not impossible balancing act to find professional help that will give you good guidance and alternatives without emphasis on their own hidden agendas or bankrolls.

The only way you will find them is to ask for referrals and then interview them yourself. All the players should be looked at as forming their own team. You need a variety of players, but all must truly be willing to play on *your* team as much as their own.

Having a Big Six firm doing your corporate number crunching lends an air of instant credibility to your numbers and organization as well as opens the door to their networking capabilities.

Having a securities attorney in the wings and on your team from the outset of your enterprise is another major plus. First, the exact structure of your organization is likely to need professional input. Once you have learned which alternatives "feel and smell" best to you, you will need legal counsel to put those desires into legalese before making your approach to potential investors. Second, the guidance and counsel of an experienced securities professional can help immeasurably in avoiding pitfalls from the very beginning and as you proceed in your money hunt.

HOW TO LOCATE KEY
ENTREPRENEURIAL ORGANIZATIONS

Private investors who are the most serious tend to hang out with entrepreneurs in particular disciplines they enjoy. Entrepreneurial organizations are a wonderful place for networking in the best sense of the word. Choose wisely so that your time (your most important commodity) and money will be invested wisely in the money hunt.

Networking with other business people, including other entrepreneurs, investors, direct business affiliates, and professional financial providers, is not to be confused with passing cards back and forth.

The networking that you can and should do directly takes time because it is about developing real relationships. Those relationships that are formed only for your own personal motives are doomed to failure.

Whether it feels like it at the moment or not, you *do* have resources to share with others, even others in a situation similar to your own. If you want open communication and help from those with whom you associate, you must be willing to provide it to them in turn.

The more shortcuts you take to get to the partners you want, the greater the risk that relationships will be shaky and not able to sustain any serious setbacks. These are the shortcuts you cannot afford to take.

Networking, in the finest sense of the word, is about doing favors that are meaningful for one another. It is more than talk. It is more of a form of tit for tat, only not always directly related to an immediate expectation of return for doing a favor for the other party.

For example, when you accomplish something meaningful for another, be it giving that person a referral, a connection to a source such as a marketing or a manufacturing person or organization, you are beginning to build your own network.

Mutually exchanged "favors" occur over a period of time. All parties involved benefit . . . over a period of time. You have missed the point if you expect an immediate response after helping a funding source. It might be weeks, months, or years later that your "favor" gets returned. And often it is not a direct connection, but it will come through third parties in the network developed by your contact.

Remember: The best way to build a strong network is to do things for others without immediately asking them to do something for you. When you do this, in time they want to help you.

Thus, tapping into key partners, whether in the legal firm you deal with, the accounting firm that represents you, outside professional advisors and consultants, business and professional associations, and other businesses and entrepreneurs you are in contact with, is the surest road to success for both capital infusion and for necessary and important business referrals.

Your ultimate success in this arena will be a direct result of your sincere efforts. The time you give to building a network of relationships that you intend to maintain and enrich over time will be the best long-term investment you will make for your own benefit and that of the organization you are building.

Networking at a level commensurate with your long-term goals and plans for growth and development will require that you build relationships with people powerful and connected enough to help you achieve those goals. Choose the organizations and the individuals with forethought, asmuch as possible. The quality and depth of character of each will eventually be reflected in the business decisions of your endeavor.

To move among those you most want to become your future partners (in the global sense of the word), you should be prepared to spend some serious out-of-pocket money and considerable time. Joining the right clubs and associations; attending the conferences most likely to yield positive results; vacationing in locations and times that appeal to the level of people with whom you want to associate all take money and planning. To do this well calls for your serious commitment to your cause.

Real networking is going to take years. You can shorten the time required to build these lasting relationships by being aware of what angels usually look like.

Because angels rarely announce themselves to the outside world but are known well to their own friends and network, you can make some reasonable assumptions about those potential sources you meet by checking their traits against the following list.

20 PRIMARY TRAITS OF ANGELS WHO FUND PRIVATE ENTERPRISES

Over the past two decades those who fund prepublic rounds of financing for entrepreneurial companies have generally fit the following description. While this description is certainly in flux as more women, minorities, and young, successful business owners enter the fray, the general statistics are good guidelines as you formulate your own "Most Wanted" poster.

1. Over 90 percent are male.

2. Typical age range is between 40 and 60.

3. Most hold master's and/or multiple collegiate degrees.

4. Annual income levels range between $125,000 and $250,000.

5. They invest one to three times a year.

6. They invest in projects within 300 miles of their home more than 75 percent of the time.

7. They expect the project or company to allow liquidation (or at least control) of their capital within five to seven years.

8. They are seeking a rate of return between 20 and 40 percent annually.

9. They prefer technologies and disciplines they are familiar with.

10. They rarely invest in more than 10 percent of the total deal.

11. They like early-stage, but not start-up, companies with explosive growth potential.

12. Their primary motivation is a high rate of return. Secondary is involvement.

13. They accept on average 3 of every 10 deals they are offered.

14. Their personal motivation is a consulting or board membership role.

15. They usually learn about deals through associates and friends.

16. They refer your program, once invested, to other associates and friends.

17. They like to be in the company of other sophisticated investors and investment banking groups. So they like to know who they are in partnership with in your venture.

18. Most have prior start-up experience of some sort, either directly or indirectly.

19. Their typical investment amount is $25,000 to $50,000 per deal, more if approached in later rounds of financing.

20. Most report favorable experience in such private investing (over 70 percent positive) and would like to do more.

Once you know what angels look like, all you need do is give them what they want and the money can be yours. Never forget though that first and foremost, individual angels are seeking monetary return. Corporate investors in this category are often seeking strategic alliances or entry into technological breakthroughs in addition to or in exchange for return on their investment.

Following are a few other tips before you approach angels, now that you know where to look and what they are likely to look like:

1. If you are seeking less than $500,000, most of the time they do not want to be bothered.

2. If you are a pure start-up, ditto.

3. Because the rate of return (25 to 40 percent *or more* annually) they expect is high, moderate or slow growth rates do not normally interest them.

4. The more you can fully utilize their input and capacities to help build the company, the better. They take an active interest, if not an active role.

5. Their top concern is the quality of your management. Second is the credible market niche, third is the substantiation of the growth potential, and fourth is the realism and depth of your financials.

So you found them and you think you can meet their first demands and qualify as a "deal" they will take seriously. Now what do you need to present to make the pursuit end in dollars flowing your way?

THE ABCs OF MAKING FUNDING PRESENTATIONS

How do you close those elusive investors, assuming you want to? Keys to closing the affluent investor are all a result of thorough planning on your part. If you can keep in mind the ABCs of making presentations, you should do very well, no matter who you are making your presentation in front of.

By staying focused on your objectives, staying honest with your listeners and yourself (even when it is slightly painful), and listening carefully to the feedback, you will strengthen not only your stage presence and delivery but your organization as well.

1. *Be as attentive as a laser beam.* Focus, focus, focus on the key elements that set you apart: your management team, your niche market, your leading-edge technology, your potential for explosive growth, your value to making critical changes in your industry, society, the environment, whatever makes you the unusual, unique opportunity.

2. *Be brief.* Rambling, disorganized, or disjointed presentations, both verbal and written, do nothing to gain attention or respect. State your case in well thought out and highly organized ashion. Make all the critical points to the point.

3. *Be committed.* You and your team will be tested and retested by potential investors to determine the level of commitment you have to the long-term success of the plan, concept, and business. They are going to come at you many times to test how you will handle stress, problems, and disappointments. You are what they are buying; your commitment to the organization through thick and thin is critical to your investing partners.

4. *Be conservative.* While your idea may be just what the world needs now, is in a class entirely by itself, and has unlimited potential without competition in sight, tone things down a bit with a heavy dose of realism. Be optimistic yet realistic. No-holds-barred and sky-is-the-limit thinking is considered naive, at best.

5. *Be direct.* If there are (and *you know* there are) weaknesses in the plan, in the management team, and in the financials, address them yourself. It will be important to the investors to know that *you* know the weaknesses, holes, and problems in the plan. Dó not wait for the potential investor to point them out to you. Avoiding discussing your shortcomings does not make them go away, nor does it make them any less meaningful. Bring them up for discussion and review, then provide answers on how you intend to deal with them.

6. *Be desirable.* While individuals singularly or as representatives of a group make their investment decisions based on hard-core numbers, forecasts, market niche expectations, and experienced, seasoned management, the other critical element to their enrollments is their belief in the idea *and* in your abilities to make it happen. They want and need to relate to you. This does not mean they want to become your best pal; they do want to know that you are open, willing, and able to communicate well with them and others in the world. As a key representative of the company, your abilities to engage others will always be important.

7. *Listen more than you talk!* Another key to closing the investor is *to listen as much as or more than you talk.* Listen to your audience. They are going to teach you plenty. Your job is to be ready to listen and absorb. One of the most important lessons is to not get defensive, stressed out, or uptight when the questions and criticism begin to fly, because fly they will. Immaturity and inexperience here can be the death knell of getting the funds you seek. Keep your ego in tow, learn the practice of deep breathing and silent meditation, anything to present a calm, curious, intent listening exterior. Stay strong and committed to the key elements of your plan while staying open to insights that may prove valuable.

8. *Be real.* You're convinced. Aren't you? So how do you convince others? By delivering what they want/need so clearly that they cannot miss it. They don't want to miss it. The only way they won't miss becoming one of your partners is when what you offer them is in alignment with what they want for themselves and the timing is absolutely right. They've got to feel your passion, see your vision, believe in your integrity, and acknowledge your grit and determination. If you don't feel these things, any trained observer can tell. It is almost impossible to fake serious passion and dedication. The real thing is obvious. When they do see these qualities, and the deal matches them, you've got them.

9. *Be self-confident.* By being fully prepared, you will be able to answer whatever questions come your way, understand the motivation of the listeners, know what the strengths and weaknesses of your plan and presentation are, know what hot buttons are likely to move each particular audience, and make the best representation of yourself and your offering possible.

10. *Be thorough.* Review the highlights of all areas that are or should be of interest to the potential investor. Whatever the particular strength of your organization or plan, emphasize it but do not dwell on that alone. Cover all the crucial areas.

When (not *if*) you do all 10, you will become a "10" in the eyes of even those potential investors who turn you down at this juncture. That 10 rating means you are, above all, *credible.* That is precisely what you want to be in the eyes of all you meet.

SOMETIMES YOU MUST WALK AWAY FROM A FUNDING SOURCE

Knowing when to walk away from a funding source is an important consideration to think about in advance. You might naively think *never!* This is not necessarily true. Only you will ultimately know and decide.

Just remember, you are entering into a long-term relationship from the moment the first dollar comes your way. Whether debt or equity investors, the tie is much like that of a marriage. Some last longer than others, some are better than others, some are delightful, others are a disaster from the moment they begin.

Accepting the investor is saying "I do." Before you do, give yourself a little time and contemplate each of the following:

The cost of accepting the money and the strings every particular investor has it attached to.

The control issues.

Sharing ownership and accolades.

Unexpected demands by your investing partners.

Under what terms you would like to end the relationship (because end sooner or later it will).

The cost may be too high. The financial arrangement may (probably will) leave you with a minority ownership. Owning 10 percent of a $100 million enterprise is the same as owning 100 percent of a $10 million one. Getting to those higher levels takes more fuel than most individuals have available. So weigh the cost versus the ultimate financial potential.

The control issue is one most entrepreneurs struggle with from the time they begin to contemplate outside investment. Even with 51 percent control, however, *real* control does not necessarily reside in the hands of the one owning 51 percent. *Real* control is that of making the decisions that drive the company and direct its future.

Psychologically and/or emotionally, ownership is now shared. This can sometimes be a blow to a beginning entrepreneur. Dealing with outside investors who are totally passive is one thing, but dealing with their input, their questions, their criticisms, *and* their shared view of ownership may be another.

New management members, vendors, suppliers, and customers may be foisted on the unsuspecting entrepreneur through the new funding partners. Try to determine during negotiations when, where, how, and who may be new working relationship partners.

Power plays and personality glitches are almost always part of the equation. Again, do the best you can to assess these during negotiations.

If or when it stops being fun and the thrill is gone, so, too, is the driving intangible that motivates the founding partners.

The strategy for investor exit will be a major discussion point during the negotiations. If the strategy for investor exit differs from what you foresee for yourself, or what you had in mind for all participating parties, the conflict needs to be confronted head-on and at least mentally resolved before you proceed.

This is often the point at which you as a founder are likely to go through an eye-opening experience. By determining from the beginning of the business launch the plan by which the investors will exit (get their investment out) and what your exit will be, you will learn if you are truly an entrepreneur or are merely in search of self or lifestyle employment.

CHAPTER 8

Successful Presentations That Really Sparkle

A presentation is like being in the Super Bowl; you may not have a second opportunity for quite some time. You are the quarterback, the center of attention with everyone waiting to see your next play. I never assume that every presentation will go as planned and position myself for every move. I want to be flexible enough to go with the flow. My thoughts are on how I can think through and perform, not on what the crowd thinks or wants.

Michael Lucas
Entrepreneur and television producer

Presentations that get people's attention and conclude with an affirmative response to your request are the ones you *must* make if you are to succeed. If you have even an ounce of entrepreneur in you, you are always going to be engaging people to listen to what you are doing. In order to turn them from neutral to positive supporters of your endeavors, you must get their attention and have them connect with you on some level. Your objective should be twofold:

1. To create enthusiasm in your listeners for who and what you are.
2. To create an opportunity for your listeners to see themselves in the picture of your enterprise.

Realize that the potential investors listening to your pitch have the Missouri attitude of "show me!" The very fact that they will listen to you is testimony to their interest in what you have to offer, but it is a long way from interest to putting money in the bank.

Your task is to get from point A (at least some level of interest on the part of your listener) to point B (investment capital in your company's bank account) in as straight and fast a line as possible. To do that, you must apply principles of effective presentation. This comes on top of a well-conceived, readily executed plan for a dynamite product or service.

In other words, the presentation should be the icing on the cake. After all, it is the icing that makes the first impression on the world and transforms a plain cake into something more enticing. The important things to remember are these:

- Some companies have nothing but great icing to offer.
- Others have great cake (content) but fail to entice interest because they don't look, smell, or initially taste as good as their competition in the first category.

Companies can fall into either category. While it might seem unlikely, some that fall into the first still get funded.

It is often the first kind that attracts attention and funding more readily than the cake. But these companies (those that are nothing but icing) usually fail to deliver on their promise. Unfortunately, the "cake" companies are frequently overlooked or passed by simply because they failed to make a reasonable effort to put an attractive cover on their offering.

In some circumstances, companies devote their major effort, resources, and talent to presentations that are absorbing and memorable. Usually, however, entrepreneurs sold on the validity and viability of their ideas believe that the product, service, or mere mention of break-through thinking and/or technology will bring in the money needed to take the enterprise to the next level.

Those companies and entrepreneurs who fall into the first category outlined here should concentrate their efforts on developing their ideas, business plan, management team, sound financials, and structuring. Those in the vast majority who make up this second category need to learn something from their brothers and sisters who understand the art of presentation. Great ideas and potentials are left on the drawing boards if not presented to the capital markets with some flair.

There are some important guidelines to making presentations filled with the appropriate content and delivered with appealing wrapping. Following are 10 of the most important rules to remember about presentations:

1. *Sometimes in the most important of circumstances you will have one chance and one chance only to make your plea.* While you may be given a second chance in some cases, often the sources you most desire are available to you multiple times only if you pass muster in your initial presentation. Presen-tations to the most desirable sources are your opportunity to enroll these individuals and groups in your vision, extending that enrollment to the many contacts they have.

Don't forget the hidden downside of getting in front of your most important potential sources. Presentations to your "silver and gold bullet" sources always have far-reaching effects that can either help or hinder your endeavors.

If the first impression you leave with these key sources is weak, incomplete, unengaging, hesitant, or just plain disastrous, it will have an effect far beyond the parties privy to the direct presentation. Often powerful sources you have addressed do not immediately or openly share negative or detached responses with you. When you later address other sources known to them, you may not even be aware of the impression that has preceded you. You will have an unspoken barrier to climb. That is why you need to pay attention to the second rule.

2. *Always be prepared to make a solid, succinct presentation that clearly represents you.* There will be times when you least expect to be making a critical presentation and the opportunity arises. You should always be prepared to make at least a B+ presentation. Even when exhausted, frustrated, or simply caught off guard because of the setting, be prepared to represent yourself and your plan with aplomb. A surefire positive response, even if funds fail to materialize, will come from such people when you show you are ready on a moment's notice to represent yourself.

An example of this happened to an associate of mine recently. He was attending a business conference that included a number of speakers who covered a wide variety of business issues. A keynote speaker was one of his lifetime idols, Wayne Huizenga, owner of the Miami Dolphins and founder of Waste Management Systems and Blockbuster Video. After Huizenga's speech Mike was included in a small group of individuals who had the opportunity to meet Huizenga personally and have a few private moments. He had his opportunity! In a short two minutes he presented his idea. Huizenga indicated that investing at this early stage was not of interest to him, but as the idea developed and reached the point of revenue generation, to give him a call and then he handed Mike his card.

Obviously, Mike handled his unexpected opportunity well!

As in Mike's case, in these moments there is no one to rely on other than yourself. Quickly read the physical and emotional situation in which you find yourself. Then carefully choose what you wish to highlight.

Remember this is an unexpected moment—often for them as well as you. You want to garner their interest and allow you an opportunity for a full presentation in more traditional format and surroundings later.

To do this with consistency in all unexpected settings, you must learn to assess the settings of each encounter quickly for its unique timing and opportunity. Listen carefully when introduced and ask questions to help you determine the position, outlook, and other related interests of the parties present. Once you have at least this modicum of information, you can far more effectively relate the key features of your offering that you want imbedded in their memory banks.

3. *Do not expect to get all you seek in just one presentation.* Your task, once you have started on the capital hunt, is to establish a level of interest on the part of your listeners that more often than not leads to funding. Ideally, you want all parties to whom you present to become resources to your organization in one way or another. If they do not become your capital partners, then at a minimum you should seek contacts that can prove helpful in any of the many business activities they are engaged in.

It is important to keep in the forefront of your mind that only by engaging their interest in your first presentation will your listeners allow you the opportunity to come back again. To ultimately get funds in hand usually takes months and many presentations.

It will help you to remember that this presentation business is much like the dating game. A first date (presentation) may or may not lead to marriage. Blind and first dates sometimes conclude with hasty marriages. So, too, do some poorly planned and/or prepared presentations lead to investment partners. Some of these work out; most do not.

The problem with hastily arranged partnerships is that the principal players simply don't know enough about one another to clearly establish a working relationship that will last. Expectations are rarely clearly and completely expressed. Only the best possible face is put on the attributes of both parties. Believe it or not, learning about and acknowledging the flaws in your potential partners and allowing them to see yours is the best policy.

Putting your best foot forward is important to any presentation. Filling that presentation with the key elements that define your unique capabilities, opportunity, and their role in it is what really matters.

Remember, if you fail to engage their interest quickly, you will rarely have another opportunity. People are so bombarded with information and outside stimuli today that their interest span is shorter than ever. You must, therefore, be concise, direct, energetic, and aligned with an interest that is important to the listener.

4. *You must engage the listener immediately—in the first two minutes of conversation.* The most important task you have in any presentation is to first get the listeners' attention and then immediately follow with something meaningful to *them.* Listeners turn into potential investors who turn into partners. From the very outset you must almost immediately answer their unasked question "What's in it for me?"

Getting a succinct presentation done in two minutes is the challenge facing every entrepreneur. As we will discuss later in this chapter, the first 15 seconds of that presentation lead to completion of your two-minute "pitch," which leads to a full-blown 15-minute presentation (the length of time most serious investors will give you).

Most entrepreneurs want to and do talk for hours about their ideas and themselves. The key here is to save that for later. If you do not get the fire and dynamics of yourself and your idea across in the first two minutes, you won't have the opportunity to expound on the many intricacies that make your heart pound.

As you will learn with practice, two minutes can be a long time. In that two minutes you can cover considerable territory. After you get the listener immediately enraptured by what you have to share, it is important to zero in on the aspects of your proposal that make you stand out from the crowd and offer this particular listener a rare opportunity *that can do something for him.*

To do this, you must learn the techniques to keep your listener focused solely on you in these critical two minutes. To do this well means using verbal and nonverbal forms of communication. The eyes are most important of all.

Your job is to convey your passion, conviction, competence, vision, reliability, determination, and teamwork capacity. Our eyes are said to be the mirrors of our soul. They truly are one of the most important tools you bring to any presentation. As I said before, if that passion is not really there, it will show.

You already possess other important tools that will be utilized in any presentation but have particular impact in those first two minutes. These are the tone of your voice, your word selection (vocabulary), and your body language. All can be used to engage or repel a listener. The lesson is to be aware of them and hone their use to be in alignment with your purpose and belief system. These are at least as important as the actual words you will say.

The key to effective two-minute presentations is to present yourself well physically, verbally, and emotionally. Engage your personal and professional resources to the best of your ability to provide a snapshot to the listeners that makes them demand to know more.

It is hoped the majority of your presentations will be set up in advance. On many occasions this will not be the case. Unexpected social and professional circumstances create opportunities to build relationships with individuals and organizations not necessarily on the original targeted list. With this in mind it is important to note rule five.

5. *Qualifying your prospects while presenting is an art form worth cultivating.* One criterion important to all would-be funded individuals and entities is determining the wherewithal of the listening audience to complete funding. One of the worst expenses of your most valuable resources, your time and energy, is that of presenting to audiences incapable of funding, even if interested.

While this may seem an obvious observation, it is ignored far too often. Do not let your own enthusiasm and exuberance cloud your ability to ask focused questions that will provide you precise qualifying information. Doing the questioning with diplomacy combined with precision information gathering is a skill to continue to hone to perfection with every opportunity.

This is a little trickier to do in those casual or unexpected opportune moments, but even there, with time and practice, you will get better. But in the majority of cases your presentations will be planned. This means you will have plenty of opportunity to prepare. *Preparation* is the operable word here if you want to make the very best possible representation of your wares. Serious investors expect nothing less.

When you get before them in an arranged meeting, they expect you to be prepared for anything they may throw at you. If you are not ready, don't set the meeting.

The presentation cannot be all one-way. You must slip in well-placed and timed questions. This is the only way to get feedback as quickly and completely as possible. This is crucial to your understanding and possible acceptance of these potential investing partners.

It will be up to you to determine which qualifiers are most important to you. Is it their cash available at the moment? Are their connections to management, marketing, or manufacturing most important? Do you share mutually admired environmental and social awareness attitudes?

Once you have determined their financial capacity, focus on what is most important to you and your core team. These qualifiers usually revolve around expectations as well as prior performance and achievement. Another key qualifier for potential partners is their capacity to assist with key connections on a wide expanse of needs.

Perhaps last on the list, but not to be overlooked, are potential personality conflicts. This is sometimes glossed over or undervalued. Just pay attention, particularly with potential lead or highly influential investors. If a conflict in personality types is there from the beginning of the relationship, it is unlikely to get better in the times of stress, setbacks, or failings that can and do come for every organization.

Remember, if you are going to make a habit of making presentations to previously unqualified prospects, you do so at a higher level of risk. I am talking here about *your* risk.

Risk is increased because you have no history of or with the people you may engage. Relationships are always built over time. Relationships revolving around capital are best when based on mutual respect coming from knowledge of and understanding of one another. Good relationships, thus, are far more difficult to establish quickly with unknown sources and/or individuals.

If you insist on this method of raising capital, at a minimum, position yourself in those locations and with groups of people who are at least likely to be candidates. That way they may have prequalified themselves at least on some level.

The next three rules all involve doing your homework on qualified prospects before you get in front of them. Good presentations before live audiences are best when they are the result of practice, practice, practice.

6. *Learn as much as you can about your audiences on both a personal and professional basis.* Insight may come from your intuition about various people you will present to. Pay attention to that intuition, but do your homework, too. The more you know

about your audience, the better your "well-educated guesses" will be.

Taking time to research the backgrounds of the various parties can pay off handsomely, yet it is something rarely done by those seeking funding.

First, taking the time to know them allows you to go into the meeting with eyes wide open. Give yourself an advantage before you enter the door by knowing more about them than they may know about you. Whether or not you openly share your knowledge is a negotiating determination.

Second, this research will enable you to relate to the players through mutually experienced activities in your lifetimes. The human experience we all share is amazingly similar, with idiosyncratic differences. Investing the time to learn about one another helps build rapport quickly and easily. If it is important to you—and it must be if you are expending your resources to get these folks enrolled in your project—do your homework well!

Third, by making observations when appropriate that are clearly based on your knowledge about the individuals involved, you are likely to impress the listeners. Your listeners may not openly express appreciation, but you can be assured it is only top players who take the time to do this type of investigative work. By having done it, you immediately place yourself in the top 10 percent position. This alone will not do the trick to get you the funds you seek, but it doesn't hurt.

Fourth, by interpreting what you learn about the backgrounds of your listeners, you can draw even deeper and clearer pictures of them. Just the mere knowledge of the schools attended, the social and sporting activities they were and are currently engaged in, and the clubs to which they belong gives you insight into one of the most important gauges of all—their value systems.

An example of this is a woman entrepreneur I know who was recently involved in negotiations with a large corporation for funding of a joint project involving the intellectual properties she had developed over the past 20 years. The negotiations seemed to her to be going in circles so she decided it was time to do her homework on some of the key players. Her research uncovered connections either through collegiate ties or through mutual work on earlier projects with three of the key executives in the corporation. Not only did the results get her to a higher level within the organization, but she also now had the ability to relate to the people in a position to make a decision.

People (especially would-be investors) may say one thing, but often they act out another. What they tell *you* may or may not be important determinants for their decision. Thus, by taking the time to determine what has been and currently is important to them, you can direct your offering into channels that hold deeper meaning for these decision makers. The lesson to be learned here and not forgotten is:

> All investments made by people (*all* investments are made at some level by individuals) involve a degree of emotion in the final decision.

Now that you have completed your primary level of doing your homework, you are ready to proceed to the secondary level. Doing this much work before you make the presentation may seem like a great deal of unnecessary work and a costly use of time. Nonetheless, if you follow these guidelines, you will create relationships that will be far stronger and ultimately less stress-ful and more rewarding. The second level of doing homework is rule seven.

7. *Learn all you can about those companies previously funded by this individual or group.* To do this homework most effectively, you need to get to the principals of these previously funded organizations directly. You want your information gathering to be firsthand, not tainted (whether willfully or not) by the funding source you are approaching.

   You are looking for what has worked and what has not. You want to understand the process between the parties as well as you can from beginning to end. You want to understand how things are seen from both perspectives—that of the funding source and that of the funded. This is one of the most important tasks you can undertake to establish both your own and the funding source's expectations relative to your own progress and performance.

A series of questions follows to begin your process of learning what you need to know on this particular issue.

Programs Funded and Their Results

- What are the types of programs funded by this particular organization (individual) most regularly?
- How often has this investor gone outside his "norm"?
- Emphasis was (is) placed on which element of the plan? Team? Outcome?
- How have the results in each case been to date?
- What are the measurable differences in bottom-line performance between the various companies funded?
- How does the portfolio appear to be doing overall?
- What is the pattern of the funding source to stick with companies it has funded?
- At what point has the funding source failed to follow through in its commitments to the organization?

Frequency and Timing of Investment

- What is the frequency of the source's investments?
- What has been the style, timing, and process for the various phases and levels of funding?
- What were the hang-ups? Why?
- What were critical decision-making points that either led to or dissuaded investment?

The People You Will Deal With

- Who are the "point" people within the organization?
- How quickly and frequently are the point people rotated or changed in the working relationship?
- What is important to know in dealing with each specific lead project manager?
- Who are the lead decision makers within the funding organization?
- Following funding, are they available to the entrepreneur frequently? Infrequently? Never?

Problems, Setbacks, Disappointments

- What has triggered significant and/or frequent problems between the funding source and the organizations funded?
- How often has original management been overthrown or or pushed to the side in favor of people brought in by the funding source?
- What kinds of resolutions have come about when various serious setbacks or failures have occurred?
- What percentage of the companies funded by this source would be categorized as "walking wounded" as opposed to healthy, growing enterprises?
- How close to originally planned and presented expectations are the funded groups performing?
- How are each (funder and fundee) responding?

History often has a way of repeating itself. What you uncover doing your homework in this area will probably show up in your own case with the funding source researched. The good, the bad, and the ugly of relationships are all part of the cycle. Better to be prepared than to be caught off guard months or even years into the relationship.

The next level of research, before getting in front of the crucial sources you most desire, is to get as much specific knowledge as possible relative to your own circumstances and timing.

8. *Learn all you can about this funding source's current available balance for funding, timing, and positioning relative to other funding groups.* Sometimes hopeful entities spend considerable time, effort, and expense by seeking funding without regard for the amount of capital available for the source to invest or the cycle in which the source makes its decisions. Every funding source has a pool of money. Some are growing and some are shrinking. Your job is to figure out for each source you approach what its situation is in this regard.

Some elements of the funding timing can and should be accounted for early in the search. Most sophisticated sources make their decisions and their funding in some pattern (i.e., considering new projects between January and June, funding in September to November). If you approach them with your new opportunity in late November, you may have missed the current year's cycle and may be in line for consideration in the following year.

You may find yourself sidetracked because of closing fiscal years, lengthy and costly audits, prior commitments, or unanticipated rounds of additional funding for organizations in the source's current portfolio. One thing no one can control but that also plays a role is a crisis of either a personal or professional manner. All of these and more can influence your timing with any given source.

By being aware of the other commitments, prior financings, and possible large obligations of the individual or organization to whom you present, you can save yourself considerable time and headaches. You don't want to spend a lot of effort influencing a source only to find that it is prepared to fund you *next* round. By failing to do your homework on their timing, you might find yourself high and dry on this round. If so, shame on you.

Your type of deal may also not be currently in vogue. If so, your timing will get little audience from these sources.

Sophisticated funding sources are reticent to admit their herd mentality in the types of companies they sponsor. They may and do expound their independent nature, research, and decisions. In truth, they run more nearly side by side in the competition for the best deals.

The instinct of wanting to ride the currently most acceptable wave is hard for most sources to overcome. Nearly all funding sources see themselves in competition. They compete both for the money-making end of the deals and for prestige in finding and funding them before mass discovery.

Much like the underwriting group for an initial public offering, networks of venture capital sources, investment angels, pension plans, and independent investors often have a pecking order. There are those among these groups who will serve as the lead; others will follow their direction.

It should be obvious to the most casual observer that it is important to garner support from sources at all levels but most of all from the most highly regarded sources. Don't expect to get their nod readily. Their lead is earned, not given. Thus, they are the most diligent in their selections.

A firm or individual who carries the lead in one particular industry group or type of offering plays a secondary or third-level role in another. The role of lead venture capitalist (as well as that of lead underwriter at the time of the public offering) is constantly rotating among the strongest players.

Nearly all potential investors, individuals and groups alike, fall prey to psychological forces, even when self-imposed. They do not want to miss the boat and appear uninformed or foolish should they fail to have an investment in what becomes a hot arena. At the same time, they want to be highly regarded for their acumen in being ahead of the rest. In other words, investment sources want to be part of but stand out from the crowd.

While your particular offering may not be considered the "in" type of investment at the moment, there are individuals and groups out there with a built-in interest in virtually every conceivable opportunity. Your job is to ferret them out and approach them when they still have money in the till and are prime to get it invested. Finding those who also serve as lead investors for a network of sources is the best option yet.

By now you should be fully aware that the better you do your homework and are prepared, the more effective any presentation you make will be.

9. *You must get their attention in order to make any presentation.* Getting attention is important, as I have said before. It can be done in a variety of ways, with varying degrees of success. To effectively get your funding sources' attention and allow you the opportunity to address them, you and your team need to put your creative talents to work.

I have observed very effective, unusual ways people have gotten the attention of serious potential investors. Some of my favorites are below. Perhaps they may nudge your own creative juices.

- These fund-seekers delivered balloons to annual meetings and public presentations being held by corporate officers whose attention they were seeking. Engraved invitations were sent for a series of special dinners with a dignitary or celebrity each desired source most admired. (Remember that research we covered earlier?)

- Another group hired skywriting to be done over a sold-out college football crowd. The message was a congratulatory acknowledgment to visiting foreign executives of a company backed by a major venture capital group. The message appeared to be from the venture capital group; it was actually delivered by the prospective group wanting funding from the venture capitalists. In other words, they made the group they were seeking look good to an existing client in hopes of getting the VC group's attention.
- The personal travel agents of several highly recognized and respected capital funding sources were invited on all-expenses paid getaway by a group of young companies seeking funding.
- To introduce themselves, members of a group seeking funding contributed their time and talents to a favorite charity of the source they were seeking.
- A major problem in a company sponsored and funded by a network of angels was solved by a group seeking funding from this and other sources.

10. *Get the potential funding source involved with your organization.* The most effective way to accomplish this is by fulfilling a need the potential investors either have or perceive they have. If all you truly seek from them is capital—nothing else—your job is infinitely more difficult. Selling an intangible (success in the future) versus a tangible (some form of gratification *now*) takes considerably more imagination, belief, and trust.

    By fulfilling one of their perceived needs, whether as a problem solver or a growth enhancer, you make their life easier. By removing or sharing an existing obligation of theirs, you gain invaluable points.

    Your negotiating position is enhanced in virtually every way if you can prove you are doing something for them, beyond just making them money. In these circumstances, it becomes a negotiation between parties much closer to being on the same level. Be it time, energy, or resources that you can leverage for them because of your product, service, or team, you put yourself in the strongest possible position to get what you want.

There you have it—the 10 rules to making presentations that sizzle and are filled with virtual reality.

1. Sometimes you will have one chance and one chance only. Don't blow it.

2. Always be prepared to make your presentation, even when you don't feel like it or are caught off guard.

3. Do not expect to get all you want with just one presentation. Most of the time, in the best of circumstances, you will make a moderate degree of headway with each progressive presentation.

4. You have to engage your listeners in the first two minutes or you will have lost them.

5. Qualify your prospects at the same time as you are dazzling them with your brilliance.

6. Do your homework to learn all you can about your listening audience.

7. Do your homework to learn all you can about other groups funded by the sources you seek.

8. Do your homework to learn all you can about the size of the bankroll available to you and the timing of its release if all goes well.

9. Get the attention of sources you want in an unusual and en- gaging fashion.

10. Put your investors in the picture of your enterprise and you will enroll them faster and more completely.

ENGAGING THE AUDIENCE IMMEDIATELY

Let's look more closely at the first 15 seconds of engaging our listening audience. The first 15 seconds count the most. Even before you open your mouth, your posture, appearance, tone, and countenance will tell any acute observer a great deal. That should tell you to demonstrate your best atti- tude and look the part of a successful business entrepreneur at all times.

I suggest that you demonstrate respect for your listener as a person by asking his permission before you talk. By doing this, you are showing respect for that person's most valuable asset—time. You may ultimately want her money, contacts, help, but it is her time that you ask for first.

There are a variety of ways to do this. One I have found to be effective and sincere is this, "Hello. I am . . . I would love to share with you what I and a growing group of enthused, energetic, and experienced associates of mine are doing. We believe we are on to something meaningful to us individually and to a large segment of the population, intellectually intriguing, and very financially rewarding. Would you allow me to tell you about it for just a couple of minutes?"

What this does is:

1. Shows respect for your listener by not just barging into a monologue about you, your team, or your project without regard for either the listener's time or interest.
2. Clearly indicates that this is an idea that has interest and support beyond just your own and that interest is expanding.
3. Expresses your love for, passion, and belief in what you are doing, and your probable know-how to bring the idea into reality.
4. By engaging the subtlety of two words, *very rewarding,* you may touch a sensitive spot, either the heart or the wallet or both.

In the first two minutes of any presentation, I suggest you attempt to get at least three *yes* responses. If you start by asking for the listener's permission before you begin, you will already have your first. If the initial response is *no* then you will have saved your most valuable commodities as well as your own time and energy in presenting to someone who simply doesn't want to hear about it. Thank the person. Then go on to someone else.

From the *yes* that comes through the force of your enthusiasm and passion, the next question I propose you ask in the first 15 seconds is, "And if you find what I have to say of interest, are you *or anyone you know* in a position to play some part in helping us?"

Two important things to note here are (1) Your question goes beyond the listener's own immediate level of interest. You are expanding your presentation to a broader sphere of influence by merely asking this question. (2) You have not gone immediately for the jugular and asked for money. You have couched your request in far more acceptable terms by asking about the person's ability and interest to "help" your idea along.

While you may be thinking capital comes only in the form of currency, real capital to help you grow your business comes in many other forms as well.

The listener in front of you at any given time may or may not be the ultimate source that responds to your query. You may well be talking to the niece or uncle of the person who could and would fund your operation or bring about the strategic alliance that could save you enormous time and money.

But you will never know if you don't ask. Always ask not only about their own interest, but also about the potential of people they know.

Remember that the capital you are seeking from these listeners may come in a variety of forms, all of which are useful. Some may actually be the currency funding sources you seek. Others may be or have access to potential managers or employees you will need. Others may be or know of other individuals or organizations that could complement your project or company and be potential partners, alliances, customers, or acquisitions. All of these are forms of capital that grow your business.

With any luck, you have gotten two quick yes responses or at least one yes and another partial from your listeners already. Remember, you have done this in just 15 seconds! That leaves you a minute and 45 seconds to complete your two-minute presentation. (What I call the two-minute drill.)

There is a considerable amount you can pack into that next 105 seconds. With practice, many outstanding presenters can actually get a full drill down to a minute to a minute and a half.

What goes into that two minutes? Basically, the contents of your business plan in condensed version:

- What business you are in.
- What makes you unique.
- Who it will take to "drive" the organization.
- The plan you will implement to make it happen.
- What kind of money (profit and ultimate capital reward) you expect to make.
- The risks you (and by association the investor) face.

Defining the business you are in and your vision for it is the beginning. Remember that building a business is much more than just launching a new product or service idea. You should be able to define your business succinctly in no more than one or two sentences.

Next you want to explain what makes you so special. While the ability to maneuver quickly in a given market may be one of your high-lighted unique features, serious capital sources will be looking for more.

Do you hold any patents or other proprietary advantages? Is it your lead time, your turnaround time in production, or your location that needs emphasizing? If the management team you have assembled is your strong suit, say so. This alone, while incredibly important, is rarely enough, however.

Whoever is going to drive the plan needs to be the best you can get. If a Troy Aikman at the helm is what you want, but what you have is a part-time advisor like a Joe Montana, say so.

There cannot be enough emphasis on the strength of your management team (see Chapter 3). This quick description of your team cannot go into the individual backgrounds or accomplishments. Instead, you want to convey depth, breadth, and successful accomplishment as characteristics of the team you have assembled.

Ideas are only as good as their implementation. A team that implements well and consistently is the one you want for your own. The ability to perform well and consistently is, ultimately, what you want to leave as the first (and last) impression of your organization.

How you are going to do what you say you will is nothing more or less than the business and capital plans to get you there. Yes, there are two.

The business plan defines the business operations, operating personnel, and goals. The capital plan defines the monetary requirements, capital team, structures, and timelines necessary to pull off the business plan. In just a few sentences you want to share how you will accomplish both the business goals and the capital needs to make them happen.

Next in your two minutes you want to leave the listener with the potential for substantial return—extraordinary return. Investors are interested in making lots of money. If you have a conservative idea that might make them a little money, even more than they are making now in safe, secure investments, their reaction is likely to be "ho-hum." People will listen to your ideas, even when they may still be little more than fanciful thinking, if they think they can make bundles! They may smile or laugh and walk away. But at least they will listen.

Risk as seen through the eyes of the potential investor or listener who may be in a position to help you achieve your goals is usually quite different from your view of it. One of the best ways to approach a quick sentence or two on this subject in your two-minute drill is to relate risk to your particular positioning of the five stages of risk.

If you are at the seed capital level, just now investigating the possibilities of your idea, say so. If you have moved beyond that to the start-up level and have documented the feasibility of your idea, you have moved further along the road and will be perceived to be less risky. As you move through the phases concerned primarily with production, distribution, and then control of growth or expansion, the risk factors lessen.

YOUR CHANCE AT A FULL 15-MINUTE PRESENTATION

So you hook them in those first two minutes. In most circumstances, you now have their ear for approximately 15 minutes. This gives you little more than an expansion on the snapshot you presented in your opening two-minute pitch to cover all critical six areas of your business plan.

In some circumstances the opportunity is immediate—here and now. In most cases, however, it means you will have an opportunity later to present your 15-minute version to the potential sources, usually on the sources' turf (at a time selected by them).

If you have something that potential investors must see to understand, you might get them to come to you. But this usually does not happen until you have passed to the next level of the screening process. If all goes well at this point, things really begin to get serious.

Whichever the case, whether now or later, this is your 15 minutes to shine before the capital source you seek. You will present an extension of the same items you covered in those first two minutes. How you break out the time will vary somewhat depending on your own case.

In any event, the majority of this time should be spent on the third item—management. Because investor sources put such an emphasis on this, you should too. Management is the key. All else revolves around the team that will make the idea, project, or company come to life and become a sustainable success.

Recognize that in your 15-minute performance, you are likely to get what you want, be it money, leads, contacts, or contracts, by delivering what the listeners want or need.

To do that you should focus your material on what they want to hear. All the key points about your organization that will affect them should be covered. This, as you will see, covers contingency plans as well as exponential growth forecasts and is truly only an expansion of details about your business plan. (You *did* seriously prepare the plan, didn't you?)

Potential investors want to learn very specific things about you and your opportunity. They are not so much interested in you personally as they are in what you can do to reliably follow through with this business. Their interest in your project is to determine what is in it for themselves.

If you do your job well in this 15-minute window of time, your listeners will be able to synthesize the information into their existing lives and quickly determine what you can (will) do for them. Don't lose sight of that.

Rather than delivering what *you* may consider most important, focus on what you can deliver that will get them to feel good about you and what you offer. Only when the listeners are absorbed enough to mesh your "deal" into their lives will they open up their resources to assist you in making your dream come to life.

There are a series of questions they are asking themselves and you either overtly or covertly. The more that are answered satisfactorily, the better chance you have of passing the initial screening and moving to the next level of serious investigative interest.

1. They want to know what the business is they will be investing or participating in with their money and/or time. A clear understanding that can be phrased in no more than two sentences is the best. Again, remember, it is not the precise product or service. Those are just means to an end. What is the business you are building around that product, service, or intangible?

2. They want to know what makes you so special. A distinct, even unfair, advantage is worth its weight in gold. They want to know what you have that is proprietary and what the organization can do to expand or build on it.

   Further, if you don't have something proprietary now or it is weak, they want to know that you can create that status. If you have such a proprietary product or service now or can create it, the next question is, "Can you defend it in the event of challenge?" If you have nothing proprietary, what lead time or other unique characteristics do you possess?

Being too far ahead of the herd can sometimes do you as much harm as good. Capital sources can be jittery, even obstinate when it comes to innovation over evolution. Having the vision and being different (special, unique) has the advantage of getting there first. Sometimes, though, being the pioneer is not all it's cracked up to be.

Pioneers often get slaughtered. That may be important to remember. While breaking into new territory may be ego-satisfying, exciting, and media-worthy, that is not your objective. The bottom line is that investing partners want to make barrels of money. They hope you want the same. Your job is to prove to them and get them to believe that their chances of accomplishing those monetary goals are best served by participating with you.

3. They want to know about your management team. In virtually all cases, investors assume the management team is knowledgeable and experienced. Your job is simply to provide the evidence that this is so.

When your management team is experienced in the industry or discipline under current discussion, your ratings just improved substantially. Nothing—youth, enthusiasm, energy, or desire—will take the place of proven successful experience in enrolling investors to your cause.

The characteristics most often exemplified in consistent, winning managements are the ones your future partners want to see reflected in *your* management team. They are:

- A history of achievement.
- A high level of energy.
- Attitudes and actions based on honesty and integrity.
- Tremendous resourcefulness and communication skills.
- Ability to analyze situations quickly, deal with the reality, and respond with urgency.

If you do nothing else well but this, you stand a very good chance of moving up to the next step of engaging their enrollment. On the other hand, good, even great, management teams alone are not the only answer.

4. They want to know what plan you will implement to make it all happen. In Chapter 3 we covered the business plan in detail. Here you want to just hit the highlights.

The most important thing to remember is to leave the lasting impression that you have done your homework well. You have thought through the steps from beginning to end.

You have identified the resources required. You understand and can address the competition. You have researched the market and its potential. You have considered the alternatives in production, marketing, advertising, and distribution and have made your decisions with careful and considered determination. You have contingency plans.

Because the business plan can and will change due to the nature of a growing, changing entity, the plan perhaps gets the least attention from many sources. It is important, but more important is your ability to convey vision, reliability, resourcefulness, and confidence in meeting the challenges that lie ahead.

5. They want to know about the potential rewards. The rewards for involvement should be directly in line with the risk of losing the capital and time invested. If you are tackling a huge problem with a great management team, it should spell a high probability of success and large reward. If, on the other hand, you have a wonderful solution to a mediocre problem, the financial rewards will reflect just that—mediocrity.

Margins, competition, shelf life, results of research and development to keep you ahead of technology and consumer wants are all part of painting the picture of profitability. Taking that to market (IPO) means a multiple of the results you can show to the bottom line.

6. They are sensitive to the risk of their money and their time. They want to know how sensitive you are to the possible risk factors. You should be realistic about the direct relationship between the potential reward and the potential risk. Far too many entrepreneurs foolishly present a picture of unbelievable upside potential for their products with little downside ever contemplated.

One way of assessing risk is to discuss the stages of the business development. These are the phases of operation from seed capital to start-up, into production and marketing, followed by management of the growth. Another approach is that of the broader scope of the business as set into the context of problem versus solution, risk versus reward.

There are three components to evaluating the risk of all investment opportunities. Every capital source has a means by which to measure these three components. While you may not know the esoteric definition of each source's approach, understanding the guideline presented here will give you a clear view of how you are likely to be rated.

The first component to evaluating risk is the size of the problem being addressed. The second is the elegance of the solution presented. Third is the quality of the management team assembled to apply the solution to the problem.

If the problem is big, it gets a high score (let's say it rates 5 out of 5). If the solution you present appears to be a pretty good one, we'll say you get a rating of 4 out of 5. If the team is construed to be only mediocre, you may receive only a 2 out of 5 rating. In this example, the source may multiply 5 times 4 times 2 for a total rating of 40.

When a perfect score would be 125, you are unlikely to make the cut and get any further attention. If, on the other hand, you came back three or six months later with a dynamite team and now get rated 5 in that category, you might find the doors opened to you again.

Conclude with the final emphasis on the most powerful thing you bring to the table. Remember to put yourself in the shoes of your listeners.

They want to know what is in it for them. Your job is to convince them that you are the answer they are seeking for their problem (which is often not having enough "good" deals in which to invest), not yours. Between the start and the finish, provide the details of how you will make it all happen.

Follow these rules and pay attention to maximizing your time, be it the first 15 seconds, the first 2 minutes, or the first 15 minutes, and you will make your presentations truly stand out and sparkle. What you deliver in the contents will vary. Just keep in mind that you always want to deliver a memorable message. Whether in a few minutes, hours, days, weeks, or months of meetings and presentations, always leave your listeners with lasting impressions of your abilities, vision, and reliability in making things happen.

CHAPTER 9

Realizing the Financial Rewards of Entrepreneurial Achievement

Moving to an environment of greater profits in
a company creates feelings of success, accomplishment,
enhanced egos, and heightened self-esteem, and
provides a real mechanism for personal gain . . . profits
create return on investment and the opportunity for cash
benefits from your financial risk taking and hard work.

> Barry R. Schimel, CPA,
> and Gary R. Kravitz
> *The Profit Advisors, Inc.*

The capital needed to fuel the engine of your enterprise has a price. Ultimately, the price you have paid for the capital needed in the early stages of corporate launch and growth will be apparent when you cash out, either through your physical departure from the company or through selling (cashing out) all or some portion of the equity you own in the enterprise. This is the big financial payoff of which all entrepreneurs dream.

In this chapter we will consider that cashing out for you will come at approximately the same time as it will for the majority of the founders and the venture capital or other capital sources who have invested.

While the song says there are "50 ways to leave your lover," there are only six viable approaches to consider for the financial exit or achievement of the financial reward for all your hard work, risk taking, and creative ideas. These are:

Going public (initial public offering, IPO).

Selling the company.

Buying the investor shares or notes back.

Selling to an investor (existing or new).

Reorganizing.

Liquidating.

Whether the company ultimately does great or fares poorly, these are the options available. Getting the highest value for both your own personal equity and that of your investing partners should be one of your key objectives from the beginning. You should plan for: (1) how to create the highest possible value for the company's assets and (2) the timing and choice of the best alternative to cashing out some of the chips to get the highest premium. To accomplish both, you need time to create significant underlying value as well as flexibility to choose the best timing and type of sale to maximize returns to you and all initial supporters.

Remember, the better you do your job in creating a company run effectively and profitably, with few major missteps along the way, the[1] higher the premium when buyers (whether corporate or public) ultimately buy out all or a portion of your position.

A few words to the wise: Now, not later, is the time to talk about the expectations your co-founders have about the rewards awaiting you all at the end of this rainbow. Once you reach agreement among yourselves, then discuss expectations with your funding sources about what they expect to get. You may find their expectations are similar to your own, or you may find they are totally different.

Determining the share of the pie you and your co-founders end up with is not within your capabilities. From the outset many entrepreneurs either try to guess or think they will retain a certain percentage of ownership (and/or control) when the time comes for dishing out the financial rewards. Few even come close.

What does need to be determined in this initial stage, though, is how the founders will split what they *do* end up with. This conversation among founders needs to occur sooner rather than later. Putting it off can be disastrous, even in the initial capital negotiations. If the founders are not totally clear among themselves, the entire deal can be blown or the terms so altered that everyone on the team pays a dear price.

If left open by co-founders until the terms of the OPM are determined, this issue will become like an open wound. While you do not have a clue of how much equity will be left to your group to share, it is important to come up with a formula that everyone agrees on. That way, whether you get 10 percent or 30 percent jointly, everyone will be treated fairly.

Also remember, people who affiliate with you through their cash, time, energy, or all three are doing so in anticipation of significant rewards down the line. They (and it is hoped you!) want their money to grow exponentially. They have selected you as their best choice to make that happen.

If your goal is something different, such as to create full-time employment for yourself and maybe a handful of family and friends, your objectives and expectations are not likely to be in alignment with those of your investors. There is unlikely to be a huge reward waiting at the end of the rainbow when the company is ready to change hands if the company's resources are drained throughout its existence. You cannot have your cake and eat it too.

When you launch an entrepreneurial enterprise, your goal should be to make it worth as much as possible. Then, sell some or all of it to reap some of the financial payback for the long hours, hard work, and sacrifice.

High sales multiples are based on successful enterprises skillfully crafted, resourced, produced, and distributed that hold promise of even greater things in the future. To get the greatest value for the work done to get to the point of exit means creating a belief in the potential buyers that the "what is" is only the beginning for "what can be."

Let's look now at the choices for turning hard sweat equity into hard cold cash.

INITIAL PUBLIC OFFERINGS

In the current boom of IPOs, this route may seem the only consideration worth noting to achieve truly significant financial reward. It is certainly the one that is likely to get most of the media attention.

Let's look at the reasons propelling the growth in this particular financial strategy for entrepreneurial America. Apart from what appears to be the obvious—huge financial premiums at the public coming-out party—there are others worth noting as well.

The Historical Perspective on IPOs

Reviewing the IPO market of the past 25 years shows some startling facts. In 1970 just slightly over $500 million was raised through the IPO market. A decade later the amount was still languishing at the $1.5 billion level. (Hardly a booming market!) It was during this time that high inflation severely affected financial investments. At the same time, America's corporate giants faced fierce competition from foreign competitors. Interest in anything smelling of financial risk was a hard sell.

In the next five years things began to move some. With successful public launches by Apple Computer, Rolm Corporation, Genentech, and others, America sat up and began to notice the entrepreneurial revolution going on under its nose. For the first time in history "small" business was being taken seriously on Wall Street.

By 1985 over $29 billion was raised. The peak during the first half of the decade was 1983 with $12.4 billion, but it fell back to $3.6 billion the next year. Another peak occurred in 1986 with $17.7 billion again, but 1987 saw a strong pullback again to $5.4 billion.

Things have gotten interesting since 1990. In 1990, $4.5 billion was the total raised. This number climbed to $16.3 billion in 1991, $23.4 billion in 1992, and hit the all-time high (so far) of $34.2 billion in 1993. In 1994 and 1995 combined nearly $53 billion has been raised.

The Exploding IPO Market of Today Is Here to Stay

The IPO market is on a strong bull market pattern. Each successive wave of IPO entrepreneurial launch is bigger than its predecessor. Importantly, what this leaves in its wake is a larger, more vibrant entrepreneurial economy for those individuals and companies yet to emerge. In other words, your timing is right on target! The boom has just begun!

Some emerging trends and players are fueling this exploding bull market for entrepreneurial ideas and talent—recycled successful entrepreneurs ready to fund and mentor newer generations as well as new interest from previously more traditional funding sources (pension plans and mutual funds).

A simple review of the who, the how, and the why helps create awareness and understanding that this explosion in entrepreneurial fever is a self-fulfilling and self-reinforcing trend not likely to falter for some time. This situation has no precedent in history.

One important substratum on which the trend is built is the funding of this generation of innovators by previously successful first-generation entrepreneurs, high-tech and otherwise. *This, in itself, is a self-reinforcing mechanism that has just begun.*

You need look only at the past 25 years to review the names of companies and their often young, always maverick founders to get a sense of the coin they reaped from their own endeavors that is now flowing into investment in the current generation of new innovators. Founders (icons even!) of those prior entrepreneurial success stories of the 1980s are serious investors in their younger brothers' and sisters' launchings today. One of the most recent success stories is Pixar Animation Studios, 80 percent owned by Steven Jobs, co-founder of Apple Computer.

Other players that have stepped up to the plate in a big way to play in the entrepreneurial funding game are the pension and mutual funds. As pension funds attempt to boost their long-term returns, they are increasingly doing high-risk private equity deals and buying stock in initial offerings. Growing numbers of venture capital partnerships are being funded by big institutions, including pension funds of varying sizes.

Mutual funds, too, are increasingly fueling the growth of venture capital partnerships and IPOs. As their assets under management explode through the investment directed into them through 401(k) retirement accounts, dollars available for previously shunned risk-taking investment are increasingly making their way to these entrepreneurial endeavors.

That answers the question of who is funding the explosion. So the question remains, Who is making these successful ideas/companies happen?

More Potential Entrepreneurs Than Ever Before

That "who" is also interesting. Those previously successful entrepreneurs are not just investing funds in the fledgling companies; they are often part of the new management team. Rarely do they lend only their financial capital to the launch of a new organism.

Also, hordes of new entrepreneurs are standing ready, willing, and able to start and grow successful businesses.

As downsizing of corporate America combines with midlife workers' itch to start and own businesses, the quality and quantity of available entrepreneurs is exploding. Also, young people, previously drawn to large, seemingly secure corporate employment, are striking out on their own in ever-increasing numbers.

Today, the best and the brightest of all ages, genders, and cultures are in search of more than a secure job and 9-to-5 working hours. They want the thrill, the challenge, and the reward of turning their ideas into outstanding growth companies. This is truly the rebirth of the American dream. Harking back to the battle cry of the expansion of America and the cry "Go west, young man, go west!" the battle cry for the new millennium may well be "Go entrepreneurial young man and woman, go entrepreneurial!"

This means the quality of the people in entrepreneurial endeavors has never been better. And, as you will recall from our earlier discussion, good people make the deals work better.

This bodes well from yet another perspective for the continuation of this entrepreneurial tidal wave. It is a self-fulfilling prophecy that things will grow and prosper when great ideas from good people are fueled with the resources they need from predecessors who walked successfully in the same type of moccasins just years before. With mentors with money now in place, the sky is the limit for entrepreneurial expansion in America. And in the not distant future that will light the fire under entrepreneurial capitalism around the globe.

Technology Makes Financially Rewarding Entrepreneurship Possible for Many

Technology is the "how" for the explosive entrepreneurial growth under way. Growing ideas and growing capital go hand in hand. In our world today, traditional leadership in the business arena is making way for mavericks. No longer does bigger mean better *or* more efficient, demanded, or profitable.

Isaac Asimov taught us that the greatest events in the history of humankind are the technological discoveries—the compass, the water wheel, the printing press. These are the ones that most drastically change the condition of the human life. In the most recent decades it has become truly amazing to see the revolution wrought with just a few grains of sand (silicon)!

Now, as we near the new millennium, with ever-increasing well-financed and managed groups of people in search of answers and new creations, more will undoubtedly occur, and occur at breakneck speeds. Learning to weigh the pros and cons of such fruitful imagination will be our next important step in adapting technology to the betterment of the human condition beyond creating billionaires of the founding innovators.

The ties between corporate size and structure to innovative creation are loosening like the strands of a rope. Smaller, less complex, hungrier organizations are being born at an astounding rate. They create in their wake new products and services at an unprecedented pace, leaving their consumers in awe at the selection of "new," "improved," "unprecedented" options.

Entrepreneurial companies are responding better, more quickly, and more effectively to the demands of more astute and knowledgeable customers. This is the house that technology is building.

The Waves of Entrepreneurial Expansion Are Building Ever Higher and Faster

The "why" of this unprecedented entrepreneurial expansion through the public offering route is that successfully funded new companies create new markets and new products. These new markets and products, in turn, create yet other rounds of successful enterprises in search of the IPO outlet to major capital sourcing.

The receptivity of the IPO explosion should be heeded by all Americans. The main reason employment is rising is directly attributable to fast-growing entrepreneurial companies. Without them, our country would be in trouble.

Large corporations are in a tailspin, cutting and shrinking. Small entrepreneurial organizations are not only picking up the slack, but they also are picking off the best of the resources, be they human or financial capital. A dynamic, revolutionary explosion of new products, services, and ideas is evolving.

Most recently, similar in many ways to the tremendous success of Apple Computer and Genentech over 15 years ago, the Netscape IPO has helped propel the Internet and the World Wide Web to the forefront of the computer industry. The successful launch of one company in a new discipline quickly brings with it others in the same industry. Witness the biotechnology "bubble" of IPOs in the 1980s and the slew of successful (as well as not so successful) ventures spawned in the succeeding decade.

Certainly the tantalizing possibilities of trading paper equity at high multiples on earnings (real or potential) is tempting for any business owner or investor. Whether or not it is the right or the only strategy worth pursuing for your organization is open to discussion among you, your co-founders, and your funding sources.

The heady returns for going public that come back to you as founders are further fueled by good, sustainable, publicly traded markets. Such a market since 1990 has resulted in 538 percent gains for new issues as compared to 84 percent for Standard & Poor's stock index.

Healthy publicly traded markets make it easier for both bringing new issues forth and for companies striking financial deals through swapping stocks. Corporate restructures, too, are helped in such times by spinning off divisions into newly traded public entities. In fact, strong publicly traded markets enhance the price for virtually all possible exit strategies by enhancing your negotiating position. Keep this in mind in terms of the timing of your exit.

Tracking the trends in the public equity markets and successfully reading the demand at a given time can be worth the effort. The Pixar IPO was originally negotiated at a $12 to $14 price point. It came out weeks later, November 29, 1995, at $22 because of extraordinary demand. It closed that same day at $39.

Reasons, Other Than Financial,
That Make Going Public Attractive

Customers, vendors, and employees often feel more comfortable and secure doing business with a publicly traded entity. Information being an open book takes a certain edge off the esoteric scrutiny required by investors' bankers and accountants.

With publicly traded stock, the company, its insiders, and its investors all have greater flexibility in business negotiations and decision making. It is a much more useful tool for expansion and leverage into other endeavors.

So Why Would You Hesitate (to Go Public)?

But there is a downside to the IPO exit. Witness the growing number of companies choosing to privatize their previously publicly traded stock. Public scrutiny does not always sit well with entrepreneurs. They tend to have some of the Old West in their operating styles. Shooting from the hip and other generally accepted cowboy practices still don't sit well with the investment bankers on Wall Street.

Another problem faced by many entrepreneurs is to predict what appears to be unpredictable. If you think doing financial forecasting in the original business plan was a drag, get ready. Once public, there is virtually no margin for error in the predictions.

If a product is delayed or the results are off even a fraction, maybe even a penny or two from analysts' projections, the stock price will instantly reflect this divergence. What's more, the stock price reaction will come with breakneck speed and just as much propulsion (be they positive or negative multiples) as the original offering mania creates. Among the thousands, large and small, that can attest to this are companies as diverse as AT&T and the Vermont Teddy Bear Co., Inc. All publicly traded companies that fail to learn this lesson are given their comeuppance the hard way when they miss their quarterly projections and their stock plummets.

Another major consideration to choosing the IPO strategy is the amount of time the founders will devote to the process. Preparing for the IPO will take six months to a year and up to 70 percent or more of the CEO's and the CFO's time.

On an ongoing basis, most CEOs of entrepreneurial publicly traded companies still report 10 percent to 20 percent of their time demands directly related to requirements associated with being a publicly traded company. Everything the company and its principals and affiliates does is of public interest once you go this route.

The actions, associations, and responsibilities of those who may directly affect the company will also be judged now in the public arena. Financials alone are far from the only aspect of the organization open to public scrutiny and judgment. Be aware of that now so as not to be caught off-guard when the time comes.

Other Considerations to Undertaking the IPO Process

One thing out of your control to a considerable extent is the mood of the market when you are ready to launch. Missing the window of opportunity is not at all unusual. Ideally, you, like Pixar, will be ready just when the time is most ideal to strike. Those windows of opportunity can be tricky to read and sometimes open and shut quickly. If you need one to make your offering attractive, you may be engaging in too much wishful thinking.

When you are fortunate enough to hit one of these pockets of entrepreneurial mania or IPO fever, the multiples you may receive can have little or no correlation to your original forecast—happily for all concerned. When the timing may not be to your liking, you may decide to wait for the next wave of opportunity or to settle for a lesser multiple in what may be a weaker, even declining, phase of the market.

To help you determine the best timing is a key responsibility of the underwriting group you select. This selection is imperative to your financial success.

Large companies rarely take a company public for anything less than $20 million. Small companies have the capability to do the smaller offerings, but they sometimes lack a following by significant analysts and institutional traders. Both of these entities are important to your company's continued market survival and growth. They play a part in the aftermarket in creating or diminishing value that cannot be ignored or slighted.

The experience of the leading underwriter (broker-dealer) in launching successful ventures is crucial. Tracking the companies they have brought out before yours and talking to the principals of those companies is a good place to begin your homework.

Good, bad, or indifferent, all underwriting groups will cost you pretty much the same. So go for the best you can. Just as with the venture capital sources, a group of companies will participate in getting you launched into the public arena.

At a minimum, get a lead underwriter who follows and understands your industry well and has a track record of success and who you can establish a good working relationship with at the personal level. The same time and effort you put into accepting your investing capital partners needs to be invested again in the search for the underwriting group to handle your IPO.

They are likely to end up with ownership in your company as part of their underwriting compensation. That means they are your newest inside partners. The same rules as before apply. Get the ones you want. Good underwriters, much as good anything or anybody, are harder to find than by just picking up the Yellow Pages and choosing randomly.

Multiple Rounds of Public Financing Are Likely

The probability of only one round of public financing is virtually nil. No company issues 100 percent of its stock on its first public outing. Also, it is not unusual for the underwriters to severely limit the amount of insider stock that can be sold through the IPO. Sometimes none is allowed. Thus, only through the secondary offerings will the stock restrictions be lifted and founders and original investors freed to sell larger quantities of stock.

You want an underwriter that knows your business, understands the unique properties you are bringing to the table, and can evaluate the best windows of opportunity for the timing of the offering. You also want a group that has the financial strength to distribute the shares as broadly and deeply as possible.

You should determine beforehand to what extent your offering is or can be made appealing to institutional buyers as well. Positioning yourself before the offering for their participation is a unique and special technique all to itself.

One more thing to consider is cost. Underwriting fees generally run about 5 percent of the gross number being raised. Some of that may be taken by the underwriter in stock. At other times underwriters demand a cash payment plus stock.

In addition to the fee to the underwriters for the placement, there are large fees for legal work, audits, writing and printing of the prospectus and other marketing materials, *and* the marketing costs to get in front of the distribution channels. You should mentally prepare for about 15 to 25 percent of the funds raised going to expenses in pursuit of the funds themselves. If you net more than 85 percent to the company in the process, consider yourself very lucky (and skilled!).

A final note on going public. Just when you think it may be safe to go in the water, reflect on the challenges even of recent markets. Securities Data Co. of Newark, which tracks IPOs, found in 1994 that eight months into the year, of the 369 companies going public, 137 were priced below their original offering price, 38 were above, and the balance were basically flat. Windows open and shut quickly!

SELLING THE COMPANY

The second most popular form of exit strategy is that of selling the company to a third party or another company. This strategy often realizes a premium purchase price because the buyer is getting the whole enchilada rather than merely a minority interest.

The difference in selling the whole company versus a minority interest is huge. The former allows the buyer total flexibility and control; the latter gets the buyer's money with little in the way of legal say or restraints on its operations.

How you sell the company should be similar in some senses to preparing to go public. Getting good audited financials is one step. Another is to use favorable media coverage to create interest in the company. The greater the visibility of the company, the better the negotiating position. Visibility through media positioning, trade publication articles and events, and industry seminars is a good way to create credibility for the company and its managers.

Now, what you sell the company for (other than the negotiated price) has interesting possibilities. You can sell simply and cleanly for cash. Great! You're out and on with whatever the next venture will be.

More often than not, you will sell either the stock or the assets for a combination of cash and notes or for some other stock in a swap. When the sale involves notes from the buyer to you, this is referred to as paper. You accept cash and paper in such transactions.

Larry Hammons provides a good example of an entrepreneur willing and able to take advantage of others seeking an exit by selling their companies to him. He bought Rational Technology, Inc., a San Jose contract-engineer placement firm, in 1994—his third company purchase in two decades. While the first two companies he purchased went belly-up, Hammons was willing to take the risk again, this time doing his homework more thoroughly. His advice to would-be buyers: "It's easy to find a lousy firm you can afford. But the owner of a good firm knows it's good. He's not going to sell it cheaply. Be willing to spend more than you may have expected."

The seller's acceptance of some cash and paper is the most common means by which companies are bought and sold. *Taking paper* is the widely used term because the promise of future payments turns out far too frequently not to be worth the paper it is written on. If the buyer ruins the business, the paper you hold is probably going to be worthless. If the security that backs it up is corporate assets or stock that dwindle in value, you are the one who gets caught short.

As a result, most entrepreneurs who sell their companies this way try to keep some strings attached to the management and finances of the company that is no longer entirely theirs. For example, performance levels are often set for new management. In the event the levels are not met, prior management or others directed by the owners may step back in.

If the cash down payment is anything less than 50 percent of the negotiated sale price, you are effectively still a majority partner. Your job will be to protect your interests in whatever ways you can negotiate until the entire amount is paid.

Usually, paper is accepted because this establishes a deferred purchase, which gives you (the founders and original capital investors) a tax advantage. You recognize income from the sale of stock only as you receive payments.

Certain circumstances may dictate acceptance of stock in a publicly traded entity in exchange for your own. Even stock swapping with another privately held company might be acceptable. Put a strong accent on *might*. This may also be a form of lunacy for you have nothing you can sell publicly and you do not make anything until you can actually sell the new stock.

The tax advantage of accepting stock for the purchase of your own company is that the income is not technically derived until you sell the new stock. Thus, tax is deferred until then. Most stock-for-stock exchanges allow for the transaction on such a tax-deferred basis.

Perhaps the very best you might try to get in one of these stock-for-stock deals is a convertible preferred stock in the publicly traded company buying you. That allows you to get paid current dividends while determining when to convert and sell the common stock to your maximum advantage.

If your strategy is to sell the assets of the company first and then liquidate the company, be careful. Recent legislation makes this a sticky maneuver. Consult a good attorney before proceeding. If you are selling the assets below book value, then liquidating and distributing, there will be only the tax on distribution. Otherwise, the likelihood is that you will trigger double taxation, which diminishes the ultimate return substantially.

Another common structure on a corporate sale is called an earn out. This means paying you an additional amount if the company earns more than you forecasted. Usually this happens when you sell the company and become a division of a much larger buying company. This becomes an incentive to retaining the current management team. It keeps your attention and focus, even though the company is no longer yours.

REPURCHASE OF SHARES

Investors are usually ready to sell their shares in your company at any time—at the right price. Your strategy, should you choose to exercise this option, should be to get a formula in place from the time you first accept their investment that allows you a repurchase opportunity.

An example is to give investors a right to sell their shares at twice their original investment back to the founders during a preset window of time, such as the first quarter of the third calendar year following investment. This is something referred to as a put—the right to "put the stock back to the company."

Normally this takes an infusion of a great amount of capital in order to buy out the investors at returns that will satisfy them (as in the example above). Usually it will mean negotiating a bank loan and putting the company into debt to accomplish it. Another means is by converting from equity into a collateralized debt position when certain thresholds are reached in the company's operation.

Yet another means by which investor shares may be repurchased is through an employee stock ownership program (ESOP) or trust (ESOT). This is in place of a pension plan and is, in some cases, a profit-sharing plan. Pretax company contributions build up the cash in the ESOT, which creates the vehicle by which the investor stock can be retired. Another way it might be used is for the ESOT to borrow the needed money from the bank to repurchase the investor shares, then retire the bank loan as the company makes further contributions. ESOTs are complicated, though, and under constant scrutiny by the Department of Labor and the Internal Revenue Service. Before you proceed down this path, consult a good tax attorney specializing in this area.

There are five investor buyback strategies currently popular and one that has limited use. They are

1. *Buyback based on a price/earnings ratio.* This is probably the most popular and the most traditional method to set a future value based on a formula easily recognized by all parties. A commonly used P/E for publicly traded stocks in your particular industry is applied to the company's earnings per share. Remember, this is after taxes. Simply multiply the number of shares owned by the investors and you have the dollar amount needed to buy them out.

2. *Buyback based on sales.* If a P/E basis won't work for you because of extraordinarily low earnings caused by salaries, heavier than usual advertising and marketing expenses, or research and development, then deriving a valuation on the basis of sales may be the answer. This means taking the profit before tax as a percentage of sales typical of the industry.

   For example, you may find that the majority of companies in your industry are creating pretax earnings of 15 percent of sales. Applying the same percentage to your own company, you come up with a hypothetical profit. Then applying the standard P/E you agree to gives you an evaluation.

   Be cautious and yet fair. Sales can be pumped up through extraordinary promotion and advertising. If you are basing the repurchase price this way, it can be costly. Because you have considerable control over expenses that determine the earnings, you have the capacity to undervalue the shares. Sales, thus, are a valuable indicator of the real evaluation. Just consider the formula before you agree to it.

3. *Buyback based on corporate cash flow.* As we have stated before, income and cash flow are two separate, although integrated financial measurements. Another form of evaluation is the one based on the company's cash flow. Usually, an 8 to 10 times cash flow calculation is used.

    The caution on this is that this method works well for stable companies but not so well for asset-heavy ones. If heavy depreciation gets added back in to the cash flow number, it can turn out to be higher than profit before tax. So watch yourself here!

4. *Buyback based on appraisal.* Business brokers abound who will provide you with an appraised value on which to base your repurchase agreement. Usually computed by one of two methods, the appraiser ultimately determines the highest and best use of the company and its assets.

    The first computation evaluates the company from its past and future earnings potential. This is much like the P/E ratio discussed earlier.

    The second computation values the assets of the company as if in liquidation. As you may guess, the two computations rarely agree (especially in this time of virtual companies). When they do not, the appraiser picks a number somewhere between them that reflects the company's value in relationship to other companies in its own industry.

5. *Buyback based on a preset price.* A predetermined price or set multiple on the investors' investment is great if you can get it. The more sophisticated the investors, the less likely they will agree to a preset price. Smaller or less sophisticated investors will, but not the worldly angels and venture capitalists. What the latter want, you won't be able to afford. What you are usually willing to offer, they will not accept.

6. *Buyback based on book value.* This is the least popular method. When this method is used at all, it is to older, more substantial and established companies. In the early years of nearly all companies, this number is low to meaningless. Thus, it is not a good measure to use in evaluating the company for purposes outlined here. Only when a company has been around long enough to establish a book value that is meaningful should this even be considered.

SALE TO ANOTHER INVESTOR

This is the one strategy that is an exit for the investor, but not for you and your co-founders. This is the alternative by which the investor capital exits and you stay, versus the other way around. This makes it an exit strategy worth considering.

Perhaps you would prefer to have a different capital partner or partners. Perhaps the initial investors (family and friends) are not the deep-pocket or connected resources you need to spur the business ahead.

By allowing an existing investor to be bought out, you may change your relationship and direction for the company. Usually the new investing partner is not an armchair variety. He is far more likely to be a new working partner, putting in resources other than just financial capital.

There are two prime targets for becoming a replacement investor. The first is a corporate partner. Corporate partners that may be initially reticent to invest in a start-up company may pay attention after you have shown some substantial progress, especially if it either relates to something they are doing or want to be doing or they are convinced it could spin into something mutually productive.

A corporate partner may want to wholly own you at some point. A good way for it to begin is by picking up a small piece from an initial investor who is ready to step out.

By coming in at a later stage this way, the corporate partner (giant or not) has an opportunity to view how well you have been able to do without its involvement or resources. It is no longer buying a pig in the poke. It likes that. It can also do you a world of good to have a partner who knows more about the marketplace and the many variables that can affect your progress and success in it.

The other interesting buyout candidate is a different venture capital partner or group. This is not uncommon because of the specialization of venture capital groups in the country today.

Early-round equity financing venture capital partners are more than willing to sell out to another fund that specializes in later-staged fundings. In rare circumstances, you may be able to sell some of your own stock to such a late-stage venture group at the same time. If that happens, consider yourself extraordinarily fortunate for achieving a bit of liquidity. Just don't count on it happening.

Keep in mind that there is a rosy scenario in which one venture capital group may buy out another, but there is also a bleak one. Allied

Capital Corporation, a venture group, lost heart about the potential of a small advertising company and was bought out by another venture group. Even after the second group came in, results still looked disappointing. This group eventually sold to a *third* venture group. That alone is interesting and unusual in that a third venture group could still be enticed. But behold! After several more rounds of financing, the third group took it all the way to a home run. The investors saw something the others missed and stuck with it. Even the most sophisticated of investors, venture groups included, can get cold feet and sell out early!

REORGANIZATION

Once again, there is a positive side to this exit strategy and there is an unpleasant one. The first is the route whereby different divisions or subsidiaries are spun off to be either sold to another entity or brought to the public marketplace through an IPO on their own.

Two good, though not outstanding, performers in the IPO market of 1995 came out just this way. Kmart brought its Borders bookstores out as a separate IPO in May and Prudential Insurance Co. sold its reinsurance business through an IPO in October. Both have shown positive momentum.

Companies that are formed in such a way may create even greater opportunity and financial rewards. The pieces of some entities can become more valuable than the whole. Each company needs to be evaluated for its own best and highest use and possibility to spin off and create new entities separate from the parent umbrella.

The other form of reorganization is through bankruptcy proceedings. This is a dirty word in terms of investment, but it is all too real.

Once entered into, all parties are at the mercy of the legal tribunal known as the bankruptcy court. It will be up to the judge to confirm or deny any plan you may create. You as founders will be last on the list for anything even closely resembling remaining equity.

In nearly all circumstances, investors are going to get, at best, pennies on the dollar. Expectations of turnaround aside, the reality is high legal expenses and little return for them once you enter this strategy.

The judge's authority is complete. She has the ability to cram down debt, dilute the equity holders at all levels, and radically alter the entire capital formation structure of the company.

LIQUIDATION

This form of exit, much like the one before it, is not one most entrepreneurs are considering just as they are setting out to slay the dragon. Often, however, it is the one selected by venture capital sources for companies underperforming their expectations.

If the company is worth more dead than alive, the decision to liquidate is probably going to be forced on you by your capital sources. If the hard assets (including intellectual properties) are worth more by selling them than by allowing you and your team to continue to manage them, this will be the exit selected.

In this process, specialists known as auctioneers can make the same kind of impact as their counterparts in the earlier stages of the company's evolvement (the capital sources and the underwriting and aftermarket groups). A good auctioneer is skillful in working the audience, the presentation, and the results in such a way that may mean the difference in getting all or a significant amount of cash out of the company versus a total loss.

To avoid this least attractive of all exit strategies, a few words to the wise:

- Establish a monitoring system that clearly measures your company's progress and positive and negative divergencies on cash flow, accounts receivable, accounts payable, missed shipping and/or production deadlines, customer loyalty, turnover, and repeat business, price points versus sales, market development and improvement or disintegration, employee loyalty and turnover, product-by-product profitability, and advertising and marketing effectiveness.
- Establish a quick-response mechanism to deal with divergencies whenever and however found.
- Listen to your employees, your customers, and your vendors.
- Watch out for the development of a hierarchical organization.
- Deal with problems when they are found—don't assume they will get better.
- Realize that more capital is almost never the answer.
- Stay calm and again enroll your best team members from all phases, including your capital sources to meet the challenge.

- Get to the heart of the problem, not the surface.
- Get ready to get tough and real with the solutions that need to happen, be they cutting jobs, closing divisions, or putting off certain forms of spending, *and* get tough with how you create more business coming in the front door.

Exiting successfully to achieve maximum financial reward is the goal of every entrepreneur. To do so means focusing on what works and what does not in running the business, being able to tell the difference, and responding quickly to problems and changes while simultaneously anticipating the future.

Great entrepreneurs and their teams do this well. In the process, they improve the ultimate value. The focus is on the long term with careful attention to the day-to-day operations and cash flow. Both must be maintained to maximize the value for yourself and your capital partners. The result is fulfilling work and financial rewards worth the effort.

CHAPTER 10

Myths That Can Block Your Path to Success

The key is to separate passive investors from active investors. Passive investors are willing to bet on your future, but must charge you for the uncertainty that you can achieve your goal. Active investors are willing to build your future based upon their considerable talents and a shared vision, because such investors perceive your future as a profit opportunity, not a risk of financial failure.

Stefania Aulicino
President, Capital Link, Inc.
(Chicago, Illinois)

Myths are the stories of our search for truth, for meaning, for significance. The myths surrounding entrepreneurs and their ventures involving capital are whispered in dark corners around the globe. These half-truths, old wives' tales, folklore, fantasy, science fiction, and fairy tales obscure the real direction and the absorbing story of entrepreneurship in America. The good and the bad of true-life entrepreneurial stories are the grist from which these myths are born.

At a time when the stock market seems overvalued and poised for a major bloodletting, the fervor and pace of emerging growth companies has never been more intense. These are favorable times to begin a new venture. Perhaps the best ever! There is an excess of capital chasing too few excellent companies and quality start-ups.

Before you can excel at the capital-raising game and feel confidence in your abilities to reach your goals, you need to rid yourself of incorrect thinking and foolish notions. Understanding the downside is one thing; being caught up in myths that bind like shackles is quite another.

10 MYTHS TO DISSOLVE

There are 10 deadly myths that can cripple a promising entrepreneurial venture, stymie an innovative project, and cloud the vision of entrepreneurial genius. Breaking through myths helps you see things more clearly and gives you the opportunity to catch yourself doing something right!

Those 10 myths are:

1. Entrepreneurs are very high risk takers.
2. Entrepreneurs are only in it for the money.
3. If you don't have the right background or the right connections, you won't be funded.
4. Entrepreneurial profiles are clearly defined.
5. If you get funded from a venture capital firm, you have it made in the shade.
6. If you fail in your entrepreneurial venture, you're finished.
7. If you've been in corporate America too long, you don't have what it takes to be an entrepreneur.
8. The initial team is the one that will go the whole distance with you.
9. Money will solve all your problems.
10. Outside directors on your board are a royal pain!

Many company founders, CEOs, and entrepreneurs buy in to the above thinking. Sometimes they believe this stuff. Other times it's in their subconscious—leftover residue from an earlier period in their life and career.

Limited thinking produces limited people. We need to explode these myths. Otherwise we will relinquish power to a false agenda and never realize our destiny because we missed the on-ramp to success.

Myth 1: Entrepreneurs Are Very High Risk Takers

There is a general belief that entrepreneurs are big risk takers. Individuals who start companies are seen as high stakes gamblers, ready to risk it all on a throw of the dice. They are characterized as type A personalities who are driven to their goals and who are willing to make whatever sacrifices necessary to obtain success.

This picture, to a large extent, got painted in the high-flying days of the late 1970s and early 1980s. Flamboyant entrepreneurial leaders, such as Jerry Sanders of Advanced Micro Devices or Finnis Conner of Conner Peripherals, gave the world a view of the rich overnight success that young entrepreneurs could aspire to. They spent freely and extravagantly, living a glamorous life much like an entertainment star. This is the picture of the successful entrepreneur the public is familiar with.

Rather than a wildcatter oil explorer or gunslinger who shoots from the hip, today's entrepreneurs are a more calculating sort. They are not averse to risk but prefer to take calculated risks. It's important for them to try to level the playing field as much as possible and to increase the odds in their favor.

The successful entrepreneurs of the past decade are far more likely to be humble, quiet about their success, and far from the lights of Broadway. The kind of business they form is now the backbone of our country's economic foundation. Employment is rising precisely because of fast-growing entrepreneurial companies.

Each successful entrepreneurial company has an effect on the economy that forces the rest of the world to sit up and take notice. Not until the tremendous market reception of Genentech was the biotechnology industry truly launched. Netscape has just done the same for propelling the Internet and the World Wide Web.

Today's effective entrepreneurs do their homework and do it well. They know their competitors, their market, their profit margins—in other words, the details of business as it is. They also know where it is likely to go and are looking for ways of beating themselves (not the competition) to obsoleting their own products first!

They weigh the pros and cons of decisions facing them and then make the decision quickly. They emotionally and financially recover from wrong moves and/or failures quickly and have prepared contingency plans ready to implement on a moment's notice.

They are operating in the here and now but looking 5 to 10 years into the future. They not only exist in the face of chaos, but they also cherish it.

Myth 2: Entrepreneurs Are Only in It for the Money

The mass media like to portray entrepreneurs as money-lusting, greedy individuals without much in the way of morals, honor, principle, integrity, and heart. The most common myth wrongly alleges that the main reason entrepreneurs open businesses is just to make a pile of money, then cut and run.

Entrepreneurs are not shy about making money, often lots of it. But to most, it's just a way of keeping score. Today's truly successful entrepreneur, more often than not, is the one who is sticking with his or her dream well into its plateauing cycle.

Witness the money and time Steve Jobs invested in NeXT Computers. After nearly 10 years of being scoffed at and considered a has-been of the Silicon Valley entrepreneurial revolution of 1975 to 1985, it is now Jobs who has already had one good laugh as 80 percent owner of Pixar and is still there working away at NeXT, now in its second year of profitability.

I've worked with some founders and leaders of some of Silicon Valley's most exciting and powerful companies. From Apple's Steve Wozniack to Jones Intercable's Glenn Jones; from Genentech's Bob Swanson to Steve Boyle of Berry & Boyle; from Tandem Computers' Jim Treybig to Bill Hill of the winery that bears his name; money was not their sole motivation. And in most cases, money was not what drove them to achieve the heights and breakthroughs that they did. Money was only part of a much larger dream.

Every one of them has said the primary force that drove them to put in killer 18-hour days, seven days a week, month after month and year after year was not money. They thrived on the challenge! And they simply loved what they were doing.

Yes, many of them amassed a personal fortune that catapulted some of them on to *Fortune*'s list of the 500 wealthiest people in the country. And some of them have a lifestyle befitting the rich and famous, complete with luxury estates, lavish second homes, fancy cars, Lear jets, and personal possessions that smack of royalty and superstardom. But . . .

"I didn't start out wanting to build an empire," says Wayne Huizenga, founder of Waste Management Inc. (now WMX) and builder and chief architect of the Blockbuster Video behemoth, which opens a new store every 17 hours. "I was happy as a clam being able to make $18,000 a year in my first small business," Huizenga said recently to a standing-room-only crowd at the Hyatt Regency Miami ballroom during the Success Magazine Annual Entrepreneurship Leadership Conference.

The conclusion is that successful entrepreneurs set off to slay the world, rise to the challenge of accomplishing something no one else has, and, in the end, make big money, too. They just don't set out to do the latter; it is a result, not necessarily a primary goal.

Myth 3: If You Don't Have the Right Background or the Right Connections, You Won't Be Funded

Some people think, "I can't succeed in business because I lack the right background and the right connections." That is garbage! Rid yourself of such unproductive, negative beliefs.

Pop in a new updated software version that reinforces the power belief that you have what it takes to go for the gold. Belief systems are critical to success or failure because they are self-fulfilling. Self-talk will either make or break you.

Sheri Poe started in the shoe business because of an ache in her back. In response to her bulimia and chronic hepatitis, she became an active aerobics instructor. The backache developed from her high level of activity in ill-fitting shoes inappropriately designed for women. She decided there had to be a better way. She asked herself, "Why not design shoes that fit women better?"

She had no money, no resources, and two small children. She also had an inordinate amount of enthusiasm and energy. Friends and family came up with $50,000 to get her started. It wasn't enough, but it was a beginning.

First laughed off Wall Street with her plans to go public and take on Nike and Reebok, she eventually convinced one woman investment banker to back her idea. This one female investment banker made the difference. She convinced the men in her organization to get behind Poe's idea as well. They decided to take the stock out in an IPO. It sold out in a week, raising more than $3 million of needed capital for Ryka.

Myth 4: Entrepreneurial Profiles Are Clearly Defined

It's a misnomer that entrepreneurs come in one shape, one size, and one gender. It will take a decade before the statisticians can provide us with a new profile, but I can tell you from personal observance: *Entrepreneurs today come in all ages, both sexes, all races, and from all cultures.*

We are in a global economy today that is just beginning to heed the power and import of the entrepreneur. From the downsizing of corporations to the burgeoning growth of home-based businesses, we are in the midst of an entrepreneurial explosion of activity unparalleled in history.

The mistaken conclusion is that if you don't fit a particular profile, your chances of success are dim and negligible. The traditional entrepreneurial profile is the one we discussed earlier in the book. Today those elements that comprise the "new" profile are undergoing considerable redefinition and expansion.

Witness two titans of business in the 1990s. One is Anita Roddick, founder and CEO of the Body Works. Another is Wayne Huizenga. They could not be more different in backgrounds, outlooks, plans for the future, or types of business.

Yet both (and hundreds of thousands following in their footprints) are highly successful entrepreneurs today. Find a niche and fill it. That is a common phrase if you are in search of a business to be in, whether now or next year. The personal traits that are necessary to attain success are found on the inside, not the outside!

Some things Roddick and Huizenga share that may be underlying reasons prompting more of today's entrepreneurs are the following:

- They do not take their companies lightly.
- They don't take capital lightly either.
- Typically, there is some form of childhood deprivation (or the perception of such deprivation) that drives them. Most often it is physical, cultural, or economic.

- The majority of entrepreneurs respond that their mothers were the most dominant influence in their early lives.
- There is a high degree of guilt associated with entrepreneurs for having left school, a "good" job, or a career path.
- These particular traits and experiential characteristics also represent artists, writers, and musicians.

While these traits are a far cry from being a requirement to become a successful entrepreneur, they are increasingly found in the backgrounds of proven entrepreneurs of this final decade of the 20th century. Whether or not these will be the motivating forces for entrepreneurs in the future is something only further time and research will tell.

Myth 5: If You Get Funded from a VC, You've Got It Made

Many young companies actually believe that when they finally succeed in getting funded from a venture capital firm, they have arrived! They pop the champagne bottles. They behave like they already have conquered the mountain. Are they in for a big lesson!

Getting any round of financing, be it round one, two, or five, is just one round in a long and grueling 15-round heavyweight championship bout. The real tests lie ahead. It's like in the ultimate bike race, Le Tour de France. You can look good in the early trials and the first leg of the race. But, the veteran riders warn you, the brutal mountains lie ahead. Only the most physically conditioned and mentally tough riders in the world will survive the treacherous climb.

It's the same with leading a fast-growth company. You have chosen to compete with major companies. You have dared to challenge them for market share. Do you think for a minute that they will surrender to you without a fight?

Of companies funded by venture capital firms, 80 to 85 percent end up in the graveyard of "the living or walking dead." This land of the walking dead is made up of companies that:

- The venture capitalists refuse to fund again in any further rounds of financing. Thus, they are left to die on the vine.
- Will end up being merged with another company in an attempt to salvage something (at least some capital for the VC).
- Will be sold to a larger entity, getting swallowed into a corporate belly with little regard for its own unique properties and culture.

A possible scenario could go something like this: Your lead venture funding source comes through, as promised, for a second and third round of financing, as your business performance stays on target. You run into a string of minor delays in the next time period that eventually leads to your failure to meet initially targeted performance criteria that are required to get the next round of funding. The VCs decide to pull the plug on you. At that point, the venture capitalists have the prerogative to choose one of the above strategies. Whichever they choose, their concern is for their own salvation and interest, not yours.

The alternatives open to you at such a juncture are not too exciting. Perhaps the best is the possibility of finding a substitute VC to come to your rescue and buy out the first group. While this does not play out very often, it does now and then. Most of the time, however, you have now been left to your own devices or "your" company is soon to be little more than a memory.

Myth 6: If You Fail in Your Entrepreneurial Endeavor, You're Done

Some folks think that if you fail in your first venture, you're finished. What a dreadful, fatalistic view of the world! And it is utter rubbish.

People think that if they make a mistake, they are through. My viewpoint is the only way to learn is by messing up now and then. One of my favorite stories in the 1980s was from Consolidated Capital, the large real estate syndicator. The company appeared to be doing considerably better than many of its counterparts. It selected good locations for properties, put experienced management teams in place, and generally thought through the series of things most likely to affect the value of holdings. Nonetheless, with the tax changes of 1986 and 1987, the company was seriously affected.

But one thing I will always remember. Their wholesalers (those individuals who "sold" their offerings into the broker/dealer community) said that in the home office they had under lock and key a list of the 50 worst mistakes they had ever made. They claimed to have written every one of them down. As each new key employee came on board, they shared the list with that person. The reason: They didn't want to repeat the same mistake twice; they would rather make new mistakes than keep doing what didn't work before.

Walt Disney went bankrupt four times before successfully launching what has become the world's largest entertainment empire. What a loss to us all if Walt had given up after his first four tries.

Myth 7: If You've Been in Corporate America Too Long, You Don't Have What It Takes

There is a popular myth that if you have spent too many years in corporate America, you don't have what it takes to succeed as an entrepreneur. That is a lot of bunk!

Some people have not made the transition from Fortune 1000 company to small start-up. But we can point to thousands and thousands of women and men who have successfully crossed the chasm and built strong and vibrant companies.

It took some readjusting for sure. Forget the legions of professional staff, middle management, supervisors and technicians, secretaries and accounting department people, and so on. When you start your own firm, you may have to make your own coffee, word process your own letter, pick up and answer the telephone, and actually get out there and do some real work!

Max Palevsky's story is one to give heart to both corporate managers and university professors alike. Originally aspiring to be a university professor after getting degrees in philosophy and mathematics, Palevsky decided that academic life was too slow for him. He became a staff mathematician for Northrup before founding a computer division for Packard-Bell.

He urged the parent company to spin off his division into a new company but it refused. So he decided to do it on his own. With Bob Beck, a Packard-Bell colleague, and Arthur Rock's backing, they started Scientific Data Systems to make small mainframe scientific computers.

Their timing and strategy was impeccable. The federal government became their largest customer. Few limits were placed on their enthusiastic spending for the space program. As a result, SDS appeared to have an unstoppable earnings trajectory. Palevsky and Beck leveraged off of this particular feeding frenzy and sold the company to Xerox for nearly $1 billion. Palevsky's share, worth close to $100 million, made him the largest Xerox shareholder for years.

Myth 8: The Initial Team Is the One That Will Go the Distance

Many of us have a very naive, innocent, simplistic notion that the initial core team we assemble to build the company in the early months and years will be the same team that takes us the distance to our ultimate goal. That sounds good in theory and in daydreams, but in the real world, that's rarely what happens.

People change their goals, their desires, their agendas, and—most crucial—they also change their perception of how the company is doing and the direction in which it is going. And what results is disappointment, disagreement, discord, and demoralization. These are the red flags warning of disaster. You must pay attention to these signs.

There is a real art to consolidating your core team members and getting everyone to pull in the same direction. It takes patience, strength, wisdom, and large doses of humor to survive. At times, you will think that instead of being a business leader, you are a nursemaid, priest, psychiatrist, social worker, kindergarten teacher, and mediator. You are!

At times you have to be cheerleader, prison warden, benevolent dictator, court jester, class clown, best friend, mentor, and family court judge. All this can drive one to drink, to curse, and even to madness! At such times, remember that it was your choice to be an entrepreneur.

Going through the process with the team members who support you and your decisions is the key to success. Conflict is inevitable. Alignments change as people's own lives do. Getting everyone to agree for even a nanosecond can sometimes be like pulling teeth.

Just keep in mind, whatever the decision, that getting agreement from every single one of the core team or the managing team rarely happens. When it does, it will change virtually the moment they leave the room. When those conflicts grow too intense, the directions too diverse, or the reality of the day-to-day existence of the business too frustrating, players will depart. New ones will always be standing in the wings somewhere.

Myth 9: Money Will Solve All Your Problems

Another major myth is thinking that money will solve everything. Many entrepreneurs think that if they only had sufficient funds, then everything would be hunky-dory.

But I have often witnessed the complete opposite. I have seen many companies strangle on having too much money. When you are given too much funding and large budgets, it's too easy just to spend the money. Instead of throwing creativity and innovation at a problem to come up with breakthrough solutions, the temptation to throw money and hope it will do the trick is often too great. And you can zip past those million dollars real fast.

Too many of those joyrides end up in smoking ruins on the side of the road. You can blame the driver, or the road conditions, or the weather . . . Often, we fail to address the real culprit: overinflated budgets.

I am a firm advocate of bootstrapping. There is nothing wrong with learning to bootstrap your company from one stage to the next, from one project to the next. This process teaches you to get the most out of your resources and skillfully maneuver with modest or little capital. This will prepare you for the major obstacles and challenges that lie ahead.

Myth 10: Outside Directors Are a Royal Pain

Many company founders, CEOs, and presidents grouse about having outside directors on the board. They are concerned about control and direction of the company. They do not want to lose control or management authority of the enterprise they have started.

So it is not uncommon to witness them deliberately stacking their board of directors with insiders, family members, close friends, and senior management from within the ranks of the firm. Initially, this board structure may seem to work.

Oh, it's so easy to preach to the choir. They applaud your every move. They second your every motion. They enthusiastically support your every initiative. And while you have achieved a temporary peace and an easy consensus, what you may have also done is sown the seeds of decay, destruction, and conflict of interests, and crushed any independent judgment or creative leadership.

That may have been fine in the quiet, sedentary 1950s; in the colorful, activist 1960s; in the mass pop culture of the 1970s; and in the go-go markets of the 1980s. But in the chaotic, ultracompetitive, global corporate warfare of the last decade of the 20th century, such a permissive, controlled board can spell defeat and failure in a split second of history.

In my years of working with various fast-growth companies, I have seen this mistake made over and over again. Getting an outside perspective is crucial to your long-term survival. Disagreement, even heated debate, is not the end of the world.

Broadening the market for your particular product or service means looking at it through new eyes, thinking laterally (in new ways that stretch your imagination). Put together possibilities that previously may not have been conceived to produce, distribute, or build customer satisfaction in ways never accomplished before.

As an entrepreneur, you will normally appeal only to the top two tiers of the pyramid of potential buyers: those who want what you have to offer and those who can be convinced they want it. That is like touching the tip of the iceberg. What lies below the water is what represents the broader markets.

A good example of this happened to one of our associates in Texas recently. His company produces drinkware that lights up through fiber optics in the base. The lateral thought we came up with was to produce a line of glassware for florists. Voila! An entirely new line of customers through the tweaking of an existing product.

Myths spring from the road map of experience drawn by people who have traveled it. They begin when people tell stories about their experience and embellish them. Our imaginations are nourished by them; they become part of the culture we call entrepreneurship.

Those myths that hold you back need to go up in smoke; those that tickle your fancy or spur you to greater heights you can help keep alive. One of the newest is: If you are a brilliant young software designer or Internet junkie, join forces with an established, seasoned entrepreneur and the world will be your oyster. The success stories of 1995 for both NetScape and Pixar will sustain myths of riches, power, and influence for all generations to aspire to.

CHAPTER 11

Secrets of the Financial Temple

The role of investment bankers in this world, generally, and in the business world, specifically, is one of the great mysteries of the universe. The simple fact is that you don't hire investment banks, you hire people—or in some cases, a person.

Reginald F. Lewis

Venture capitalist, Chairman, CEO
TLC Beatrice International Holdings, Inc.

By now, you are well aware that there is no single right way of getting funding to achieve your goal of building a successful enterprise. Bootstrapping and strategic partnering work well for some; for others these techniques may be too slow or too stressful if the "right" partners are not found. For others, still, the earliest round or rounds of capital needs may be met through bootstrapping followed by more traditional rounds of financing such as we have discussed.

Getting started with the funds of family and friends is common. Building a truly entrepreneurial company—not just an employment opportunity for family and friends—is rarely done this way entirely. But it has been—and successfully.

Going on-line with the Internet or surfing for investors through America Online, CompuServe, or Prodigy may be the answer. If not that, then perhaps government grants or loans.

Small capitalization offerings (SCOR) up to $1 million or reverse mergers each have their own pluses and minuses. One or some combination may be right for you.

For others, seeking venture capital money early in the game has proven to be the best route to conquer a fast-moving competitive environment and take the lead. For some, early venture capital investment has turned into a horror story.

And what of the pinnacle of the capital raising process—going public? Is it always what it's cracked up to be? Not according to some sources. What can be good for the gander can sometimes kill the goose.

Ultimately, only you can choose the partners to be your funding sources. When and whether you accept their hard dollars, exchanged or bartered resources, or sheer sweat equity investment, the decision will affect your life and the lives of all critical players attached to your dream from that moment forward.

Here, then, are some tales from the street to give you a taste of real-life scenarios in which various combinations of strategies, partners, and/or financial structuring choices have worked for others. Always remember that whatever comes your way, there will be times that all you can do is react to the events that bombard you. It takes planning and forethought to turn that around and create instead.

I suggest you make only three demands on yourself as you begin your journey into entrepreneurship, whether for the first time or the fifteenth. Promise yourself to always do the best you can.

Second, promise to give yourself enough time to prepare for the steps to ensure success. Few things in life really *have* to happen in the blink of an eye. Take enough, but not too much, time to make your critical decisions. You will find this is not a luxury but a necessity you cannot afford to do without.

Third, promise yourself to obtain directly, not through intermediaries, enough knowledge to understand your options as you proceed. An uninformed decision is nearly always a bad one.

Making decisions on financing, partnering, and structuring should not be done lightly or in haste. By fulfilling all three promises to yourself, you will bring forth your best creative abilities, intuition, and vision. That is what entrepreneurship is all about!

It is highly unlikely that you will choose to use only one of the methods we have discussed in this book. Be it bootstrapping, partnering and strategic alliances, venture capital, reverse mergers, or going public, all are likely to be contemplated at some point in your entrepreneurial career. In fact, combinations of the different strategies will probably become reality as your organization grows to meet the demands of the new millennium.

BOOTSTRAPPING

Bootstrapping refers to pulling oneself up by their own bootstraps. The technical definition is to develop solutions through individual initiative, effort, and energy with little or no outside assistance. The many forms and techniques of this are as wide as your imagination will allow.

The aura of bootstrappers is one of moderation, skill, even wisdom. They have an inordinate capacity to make much out of little. Perhaps their greatest strength is their ability to develop a healthy respect for resources in any form. They have developed a clear notion of their own best talents through self-reliance and making a habit of frugally approaching each situation.

While there are many forms of bootstrapping, the most popular form is to borrow on credit cards. Among thousands who have launched their company this way, Karen Behnke financed her company PacificCare Wellness Co. in its early days by borrowing on all her credit cards and selling personal belongings. It took a major chunk of time each day just to figure out where the money would come from to keep the bills paid. One way or another this is true for virtually all entrepreneurs, bootstrappers or not.

An Alternative Boostrapping Technique

As an alternative to using every last nickel of cash or strapping yourself to the maximum credit card limit you can achieve, one often-overlooked bootstrapping technique is that of borrowing against the cash value of life insurance. Today, according to the American Council of Life Insurance in Washington, D.C., there is more than $11 trillion worth of life insurance in force. While only whole life policies carry any cash value, they usually do so after only three to five years.

The benefits of this form of financing are simple. You can keep your insurance in force while borrowing up to as much as 90 percent of the policy's cash value. The cost is good, too. The rates are closer to mortgage loan rates, a good 30 to 50 percent less than credit card loans. The only problem is that if you die, the proceeds to your heirs will be diminished by the amount of your loan.

Learn All You Can about Bootstrapping Methods

Rick Rueb, founder of Rikken Inc., started his journey by attending seminars given by the Small Business Development Center (SBDC) at Northeastern State University in Tulsa, Oklahoma. He got a backer, an investor willing to front him for $500,000, easily, maybe too easily.

His dream of building a company to design men's apparel with custom-made materials looked like it was about to come true. Off to New York he went in search of the custom-woven fabrics he wanted. While there, his backer called to give him the bad news. A setback in his own dealings meant he could no longer finance Rick.

After negotiation, a compromise was reached. The investor agreed to $60,000 and maybe more, if and when performance was to his liking.

Time for bootstrapping. Rick had been given a straw through which to breathe and he had his American Express card. He began in his home, as do many other enterprising entrepreneurs. After operating there for two months, he rented a 600-square-foot office. He was determined to stretch that capital as far as it would go.

Rather than spending upward of $30,000 for his trade show booth, he made his out of cardboard rectangles bound with twine. For props he used old corrugated aluminum and snowshoes. His display racks were made of plumbing pipes and the tables and metal camping chairs had bandannas tied around the legs. The booth was named one of the best of the show.

Today Rikken is selling millions of dollars of merchandise to the likes of Macy's and Nordstrom's. But the battle for financing continues, and Rick continues to ply his bootstrapping ways.

Bootstrapping as a Way of Life May Be a Habit Worth Keeping or One to Give Up When the Time Is Right

One of the hardest lessons for bootstrappers to learn is when to let go of the habits that worked so well in the early days. As companies expand from dozens to thousands of workers, techniques that worked when things were small will not always work when sheer numbers and size dictate more complex solutions.

The basic character of the lead entrepreneur often has a tendency to stick with the company throughout its corporate expansion. Resourceful thinking and self-motivation are badges of honor worn proudly by more than one entrepreneurial icon.

An example of this was the dilemma facing Ben Cohen of Ben & Jerry's. To find his own replacement, the company could no longer stick to the policy that no one in the company could make more than seven times the salary of the lowest-paid worker. A policy that had served the company well in its initial years did not work any longer because the job called for a high-echelon executive who would be paid in line with other top-flight executives running comparably sized organizations.

Resourceful Thinking and Self-Motivation Are Bootstrappers' Characteristics Worth Keeping

Dick Egan is hardly a household name, but he probably should be. That was never his goal. He grew up in humble surroundings, embarrassed about his father and family. He played sports in leagues sponsored by the Catholic Youth Organization. He went to a commuter college and studied a subject that did not particularly interest him but one he hoped would land him a decent job one day.

He has a "thing" about IBM. That's the company he measures himself by, the one he wants to beat. The "thing" started with a weekend when he and two college buddies went to take the IBM employment test. They had done their share of partying the night before and were told on entering the room that perhaps they were not IBM material. They took the test anyway. They got the three highest scores in the group and promptly told IBM good-bye.

After getting his experience at Honeywell, working on his graduate degree at MIT (although he did not get the graduate degree), and working at Cambridge Memory Systems (Cambex), Egan founded EMC in 1979 with the capital he hoarded from his years of traditional employment. With that and help from his friend Roger Marino, he was launched.

When it started, they had no product and no defined market, just a great deal of chutzpah and belief in themselves. So they did what they had to do to get themselves where they eventually wanted to be. What they wanted was to design, develop, and engineer something high-tech. What they did to keep the cash flow going was sell office furniture.

Today EMC is a recognized leader in the bundling of arrays of disks to handle the massive storage and rapid-retrieval demands of IBM mainframe users. He runs the company with an iron fist, breaking many of the "new rules" of the game by employing family throughout and keeping control of the board. In a world without rules, Dick Egan lives by his own.

PARTNERING (STRATEGIC AND OTHERWISE)

Partnering—with whom, why, and for what purpose? Those are the key questions all entrepreneurs should be asking themselves.

One form of partnering on the rise is that of spouses and significant others. What has been an accepted form of partnering in the creative circles of television and movie production is spilling over into all types of companies.

Such partnering relationships in the past have mostly been construed to mean a spouse working for, not with, his or her partner. But times are changing. Partners in and out of the board room are beginning to gain notice because they are beginning to create fortunes.

In a study conducted by Pitcairn Financial Management between 1985 and 1989, 2,000 companies were compared to create a model "family universe" (in the business start-up sense of the word). The cumulative return on investment of this universe outperformed the S&P 500 in each of the four years surveyed. The difference was between 8 and 18 percent each year.

The more traditional form of partnering, or at least the one less controversial and more readily recognized, is that of the corporate partnering arrangement. Often between a larger entity and a smaller, more entrepreneurial renegade, these arrangements have much to offer the entrepreneur by stretching capital in multiple ways.

For example, in today's quickly developing communications medium of the Internet, you need a scorecard to keep track of the new alliances being formed; they are happening so quickly. Alliances and partnering are being done by large and small corporations alike and filling the dance cards of each with multiple partners. Witness the numerous deals being struck by Microsoft—with AT&T, America Online, CompuServe, and so on.

Partnering and strategic alliances can be a powerful strategy. Through such relationship building, business owners can build their equity faster. They are perceived with a broader, deeper base of operations and distribution.

This, in turn, creates a perspective that the quality of their organization has somehow improved overnight. In aligning with more powerful and recognizable businesses, the rub-off of "brand" recognition and prestige becomes a real asset, one that you can take to the bank.

Perhaps the most powerful reasons for partnering are the depth and quickness of building credibility and authority in a given discipline. In creating alliances, lateral endorsements are effected that might otherwise not be available at any price.

There are five major benefits of creating strategic partnering alliances:

1. You can keep your costs for marketing, advertising, and prototyping under control. Rather than reinventing wheels, you leverage off of the time, effort, and resources that a partner has already invested. The results of their investigative work have not cost you time or capital. Thus, you move much further along much more rapidly.

2. You can take advantage of economies of scale. Be it in the advertising, printing, personnel, warehousing, shelf space purchase, or marketing areas of the budget, combining forces keeps costs down.

3. As a small business, there are frequently technological breakthroughs that are ill-afforded you. Combining with a larger partner not only allows you the opportunity of working with the
   latest technology, but it also often makes it available to you
   without any start-up investment of capital. Also, as the larger
   organization gets the bugs out of the technology, this reduces the
   time you and your team may need to spend on the learning
   curve. Licensing arrangements may allow you to participate in
   the latest distribution systems that would otherwise be out of
   your reach.

4. By matching your product and/or service with others, you stand a
   good chance of snaring a greater share of the market. Cooperation
   by playing off of one another's strengths and filling in the gaps for
   one another's weaknesses can build a better mousetrap. That
   becomes more appealing to the consumer, creating increased revenue for each that might otherwise go to neither.

5. You can preserve more of your independence. When the partnering is done with customers and suppliers, sometimes even existing competitors, you acquire what you need without paying for
   it. Each retains its own identity and unique independence but
   works cooperatively on joint objectives.

But before you jump out of your own frying pan into the corporate
partnering fire, there are three key questions to ask yourself.

First, are you ready and willing to give and take with a corporate
partner? You (Mr. or Ms. Entrepreneur) are usually the one who wants to
run the show and be in control. With a corporate partner, there is definitely someone who will have a say—no armchair investor here.

Second, has this potential partner done this before? You should
want to know how well that went and why before you put your own toes
into this fire.

Companies that have not partnered before are going to go through a
dance and a process, similar to marriage, while all the kinks and bugs get
worked out. Those who have experience stand a better chance of fore-
seeing the potential problems and coming up with solutions beforehand.
Among those headaches lying in wait for you is the clash of corporate
cultures between entrepreneurial mavericks in your stable and dyed-in-
the-wool traditionalists in the corporate partner's camp.

Third, what exactly do you want in this arrangement? If you are incapable of defining your needs (wants), you are probably not ready for a partner. Maybe what you are seeking at the moment is going to cost you some extra money if you don't form this alliance. So what? If you aren't ready for the partner and don't know clearly what will make you happy in the arrangement, walk away. There is always another partner, another day, to form a new alliance.

As a general rule, entrepreneurs who either already have all the money they need or are successful in their bid for financing pay for virtually all services and people. Those who don't have it, bootstrap and barter for it. Those who can plan carefully and effectively to design a good working partnership and know how to manage it form strategic alliances.

This may be the business model that will reign supreme in the future. As the customers of the future tell you what they want, rather than responding only to what you provide, your job will be to put together the pieces of the puzzle to fulfill that customer desire.

Coming together to create these temporary alliances for profit is termed a *holonic network* by Patrick McHugh, Giorgio Merli, and William A. Wheeler III in their book *Beyond Business Process Reengineering*. They conclude that all business of the future will soon use this model.

Their model of strategic partnerships is one of independent organizations coming together to fulfill a precise function. While each has its own definitions of service, success, and customer satisfaction, they work more effectively in the holistic model because they share the same assumptions.

Applying their assumptions, the holonic pattern of partnering in the future closely resembles the stages of risk faced in all business organizations. As we discussed earlier in this book they are:

The start-up phase (research and development).

The production phase (manufacturing).

The marketing phase (customer buildup).

The management phase (maintaining and growing profitability).

This is food for thought as you consider your financial options of seeking various strategic partners. Not only the out-of-pocket costs may be shifted, but the responsibility for a particular phase of development as well.

Andrew Ha, the engineer who created BeeperKid, began somewhat naively thinking he had created something new. Little did he know that other companies before him had tried and failed to create a reliable product such as his to keep parents and children connected in busy crowds.

His funding for A&H International Products, Inc., began out of his own pocket. Quickly he moved to a need for serious capital to create a dependable and reliable product with as wide a market as possible. He enticed a merchant banking firm to become his majority investor. Equally or more important than the capital it brought to the table, it linked him with a defense contractor that had appropriate technology to license to his firm.

Such a seemingly odd coupling of a corporate partner in Ha's case paid off handsomely. Creating a proprietary product with the financial backing that allowed thorough product and market testing has resulted in multimillion-dollar sales figures.

With A&H's exclusive license and sales exploding, the children's market may be the first of many. Other applications, both for seniors and for tracking portable electronic gear, are now under consideration and testing.

VENTURE CAPITAL

Getting the backing of a venture capital group may be cause for celebration or it may be the beginning of the end. The group's influence, contacts, capital, and guidance can cut both ways.

One of the best examples I know of is Alan Shugart. My first encounter with the man and his story was at Seagate Technology in the late 1970s. By that time, Shugart had experienced both the sweet and the sour taste of VC money.

In 1973 he founded Shugart Associates after having spent nearly two decades working for both IBM and Memorex. His personal experience in building the company was somewhat similar to that of Gene Amdahl over in Sunnyvale. Both were ousted by the financiers and left with little to show for their experiences, other than the experience itself.

Shugart's next project would end up leading to the need for VC money as well. As one might suspect, he was a bit dubious. The idea for the new company came from one of his former associates at Shugart, Finnis Conner. Conner proposed, and they eventually formed, a company to manufacture Winchester drives for 5 $\frac{1}{4}$-inch rigid disks. This was considered a hot new technology at the time.

By this time, in 1979, Shugart was making 8-inch drives but the smaller version, envisioned by Conner, had no competition. Their call was right on the money.

C. Norman Dion, a 15 percent owner in Dysan Corporation, a company that had been making the 14-inch Winchester disks and had only recently begun making the 8-inch version, became their backer. Shugart and Conner reached agreement with Dysan whereby Dysan ended up with nearly 50 percent of Seagate Technology, Inc. (the new company they jointly founded). They became not only the primary Seagate supplier, but also received a royalty-free nonexclusive, nonassignable, and irrevocable worldwide license to make, use, or sell Seagate's eventual product. They also had full right to incorporate it into any future computer system they might want to market in the future.

This agreement was done on a handshake. It was between two men who knew and trusted one another. Shugart had been Dion's boss, both at IBM and at Memorex.

Seven months later $1 million was raised through venture capital. Not until then was the agreement between Dysan and Shugart documented. By the time the venture capital money came in, the ownership of the company was drawn. Eventually both Shugart and Conner each was left with 10 percent ownership, worth over $80 million each.

REVERSE MERGERS

A somewhat controversial, but nonetheless highly effective, form of raising capital is that of the reverse merger. This is where a public shell company (a defunct company with little or no assets or line of business), a blind pool, or a special purpose acquisition company acquires a privately held business. The once-private business becomes a public entity with access to the acquiring company's cash, if there is any, and to the public equity markets.

The circumstances under which such a scenario occurs are most frequently those in which the owners of the public company base their decision not so much on market conditions as on whether they like the terms of the deal. The concern you should have as an entrepreneur considering this form of capitalization is for the skeletons that may be hanging in this shell's closet. Any left hanging around, especially after the merger is done, become yours!

Certainly there are tales of woe regarding unscrupulous reverse mergers, but it remains a viable alternative for companies prepared for this route. As with any other form of structuring or capital sourcing, this is merely another financial technique. The outcome in each circumstance depends on the character and ethics of the entrepreneurs and financiers who construct it.

The good news is that if you acquire shells that have cash residing in them, the cash becomes yours once the deal is closed.

The bad news is twofold. One is that you now have all the legal and accounting reporting requirements and fees associated with a publicly traded company. Second, you are not likely to be able to sell more stock to raise additional capital, at least on the public market.

Most of the time there is little support in the marketplace for the stock of the public company that has just gobbled you up. After all, it was virtually extinct before you became its dinner.

But selling your stock away from the public market in private fundings does become easier. The reason is simple. Investors can see a way to sell their stock in the open market when and if something positive happens to the company. This provides them an easier access to exit on their own terms and in their own time.

THQ Inc., a California company that was launched in 1990, was faced with an opportunity to create a much wider and faster distribution channel for its products just months after its inception. To do this required a great deal of money, money the company did not have.

Banks weren't interested. But a few months later a blind pool (Trinity Capital Corporation) was. It had a pool of $2.5 million and warrants to raise an additional $7 million. The $2.5 million was immediately put at the disposal of THQ.

At that time, THQ had sales of $3 million, hardly enough to contemplate a serious run at the public markets. Through the reverse merger with Trinity, it was afforded the funds needed to compete and explode much more readily.

A year later, after THQ was fully merged into Trinity, it exercised the warrants and got the other $7 million. One year later it accomplished a $6 million secondary offering and six months after that successfully concluded another $5 million in a private offering.

GOING PUBLIC VERSUS STAYING PRIVATE

The technological revolution is resulting in awesome innovation. That innovation is fueling the explosion of entrepreneurial companies. More companies than ever are coming to the IPO market. Simultaneously, more still are exploding behind the scenes.

Old-line industries including airlines, steel, and distribution are being reshaped at the same time as whole new industries, such as the Internet, are being born. Innovation, breeding on itself, is continuing to lead to even more breakthroughs and developments to fuel round after round of newly emerging growth companies.

Pushing the envelope with technology, today's entrepreneurs are creating greater productivity, efficiencies, and responsiveness to market demand. On top of that, they are making these strides with a cost savings that is frightening to larger, more traditional companies. These innovators are coming out to the public markets for the capital to fuel their engines like never before.

With such explosive productivity in operation, distribution, and financial market activity, a natural question is, "Can it last?" And "What has been the staying power of those who started in this boom in this past decade?"

Using the *Inc.* 500 class of 1985 as the ruler, the results are promising. As a group, the 1985 class had sales of $7.4 billion. In 1995 just two combined (Microsoft and Merisel) had sales of $9.6 billion. Of the alumni, 233 had almost four times the sales of the entire 1985 list.

In a decade that included a serious recession, a more than serious credit crunch for business, tax law changes that had adverse effects on significant portions of the economy, and a stock market that took at least one significant dive, the failure rate was not bad. An average of approximately 10 companies closed their doors each year of the decade, resulting in a 19 percent failure rate over all.

What may be the most surprising fact about these top-rated entrepreneurial companies launched a decade ago is that nearly half are still privately held. Of the 500, 201 have made the decision to stay out of the public eye and fund their growth internally or through private means. Of these, 86 percent reported growing revenues. The spinoff of existing or newly created divisions has helped fund revenues for additional expansion, such as the case of Foreign Candy, based in my old stomping ground, Iowa.

The story of 1995, as far as the benefits of going public are concerned, is that of Netscape. With founder Jim Clark using $4 million of his gains in Silicon Graphics to fuel it and a partner ideal to the purpose and time in Marc Andreessen, Netscape struck a nerve from Main Street to Wall Street. Its stock came out in late summer at $28 a share and was up over 500 percent by year-end.

Another footnote in history of considerable interest is provided by both Netscape and Pixar. Both came to the public market in 1995. Both had heavy investment as well as management direction from previously successful business mavericks and pioneers.

Silicon Graphics' Jim Clark and Apple Computer's Steve Jobs had both been there before, achieved great success, and reinvested in a new round of entrepreneurial endeavor. Double success, while rare in the past, will be the new paradigm of the business world in the years ahead. With the large number of successful entrepreneurial companies launched in the past 20 years, the millionaires made in their wake now stand ready to capitalize yet another wave of innovation!

The lessons for all entrepreneurs to remember follow.

- Commit to yourself and your dream.

While your commitment to follow through for your investors, your employees, and your customers is simply sound business, the core of commitment must be to yourself and the dreams that launch your endeavors.

- Never let failure be permanent; if you are going to do it, do it fast.

The road to success always has been and always will be bumpy—filled with potholes and nasty surprises. If you make a mistake (and you will!) acknowledge it, learn from it, and then move on. Don't get frozen by merely making mistakes.

- Don't rest on the laurels of your past success; challenge yourself to new heights.

Success can sometimes be your worst enemy, especially early success that can make you think you know how to do everything right. A few bumps and bruises are actually good. Setting new and higher goals and always having them at the ready is important; never fail to be without them.

- Keep your vision bright, even when no one else sees it.

Leadership is about bringing others along with you to new levels of accomplishment, even when sometimes it is not clear exactly where things will end up.

- Build on your successes and learn from your failures.

One step at a time is the way lasting success is built. One small success leads to another. Taking setbacks and disappointments in stride and moving to succeeding new steps is the mark of determination needed by today's enterprising entrepreneur.

- When times get tough, refuse to quit.

Don't let the turkeys get you down. Naysayers will never go away—even some of those close to you. You cannot afford to listen to the negative press for very long or it will get you off track. Stay focused and clear; pay attention but do not be overwhelmed by the negatives.

- There are always several ways to skin the cat. When one door closes, knock on other doors, until the right one opens.

Don't set your sights on just one investor you *just have to have* or one strategy that *just has to work*. Be flexible; look around for alternative routes and different strategies. Keep your mind and your options open. You are likely to need them all.

- Anticipate tomorrow's problems today; then solve them.

There is a saying that you can't grab the brass ring if you are looking back. It's true. You must get beyond thinking only about the problems you are facing today to anticipate how you can provide elegant solutions to problems as yet unnoticed or created.

- See change as your friend and build it into your plan.

Because things will change, always staying open and receptive to doing things in new and different ways is not a luxury, it's a necessity. Prepare for obsolescence of products and services long before they would "normally" need replacement. Cut your thinking about the shelf life of your creations in half.

- Change the way people think and you create new markets.

A growing percentage of new products and services are for things that did not exist a decade ago. To a large extent this is a result of technology's rapid advances. People are increasingly receptive to new products, faster ways of doing things, and are less intimidated by communications and computer-assisted change.

- Make a difference!

Whatever you set out to do, do it well; leave an imprint that is larger and more important than you. Build a legacy by making the world a better place for your having passed this way and having taken the time to build your own version of a better mousetrap.

INDEX

A B O U T   T H E   A U T H O R

Author, lecturer, entrepreneur, and investment advisor—Linda Chandler is one of the nation's leading authorities on capital formation, financial structuring, entrepreneurial leadership, and future business trends. Ms. Chandler is in wide demand as a keynote speaker, lecturer, and business seminar leader on a range of programs including management training, leadership development, sales training, and motivational topics. In addition, she has produced a number of video and audio programs, including her best-selling audio albums, *Secrets of Raising Serious Money for Your Business,* parts I and II.

A superstar in securities and investment banking, Ms. Chandler has raised over one billion dollars in investment funds for firms such as Jones Intercable, AT&T, Teradyne, Intel, Rolm Corporation, Seagate Technology, Apple, Conner Peripherals, Lockheed, Genentech, The Limited, Toys 'R Us, Sun Microsystems, National Semiconductor, and Tandem.

Ms. Chandler holds B.S. and Masters degrees from Iowa State University and is a member of Phi Delta Theta Scholastic Honor Society. She has been recognized for her achievements in *Money, Wall Street Transcript, Financial Planning, Registered Representative, Success, Inc.* magazine, and numerous other publications. In addition, she's been honored in *Who's Who in the West, Who's Who in Finance & Industry,* and *Who's Who of American Women.* Ms. Chandler serves on a number of corporate boards across the country. She is a financial and strategic advisor to a select number of emerging growth firms.

After becoming the first woman vice president at Sutro & Company, one of the nation's most prestigious regional brokerage firms, Linda Chandler co-founded Chandler/Roberts, the nation's first all-women securities firm. After two highly successful years, the firm was merged with the West Coast's largest investment banking firm, with Ms. Chandler being named Senior Vice President.

Today, Linda Chandler is CEO of Chandler Leadership & Development, a training and seminar firm; and Chairman of Chandler Broadcasting Systems. Linda is also President of Drew-Carnegie, Inc., a mergers and acquisition firm; and CEO of Learning 2000, an electronic publishing company.

CHANDLER LEADERSHIP & DEVELOPMENT, INC.:

National Office:
9832 Tehama Court
Las Vegas, NV 89117
T (702) 838-4662
F (702) 838-9566
e-mail: bizseminar@aol.com

East Coast Office:
P.O. Box 1360
Fernandina Beach, FL 32035-1360
T (904) 277-3430
F (904) 277-8809
web site: **www.LindaChandler.com**